1005001357

Healing the Hurting

Sister Immaculate Heart, Superior of the Contemplative Sisters of the Good Shepherd (left) and Sister Ambrose, Superior of the Apostolic Sisters of the Good Shepherd.

Healing the Hurting

MARYVALE

HELPING ADOLESCENTS
AND THEIR FAMILIES FOR 80 YEARS

by
Paul Vasey

CRANBERRY TREE PRESS
WINDSOR, ONTARIO, CANADA

Published by:
Cranberry Tree Press
5060 Tecumseh Road East, Suite 173
Windsor, Ontario, Canada N8T 1C1

Printed in Canada.

14 13 12 11 10 09   5 4 3 2 1

Library and Archives Canada Cataloguing in Publication Data

Vasey, Paul
        Healing the hurting : Maryvale : helping adolescents and their
families for 80 years / Paul Vasey.

ISBN 978-1-894668-38-5 (pbk.).—ISBN 978-1-894668-39-2 (bound)

        1. Maryvale Adolescent and Family Serivices—History. I. Title.

HV1441.C32W47 2009   362.20835'0971332   C2009-901692-3

"No one should be lost in the chaos of our times."

—from the Good Shepherd website

Table of Contents

Foreword

MANY PEOPLE will walk in and out of your life. Some leave footprints on your heart and you are never the same again.

The Sisters of the Good Shepherd have left footprints on the hearts of many in the Windsor community, and we will never be the same. How do you explain the impact a group of passionate, humble nuns can have on individuals, children, and a community? How do you ever thank them?

June 3, 1929, five Good Shepherd Sisters arrived in Windsor as requested by the Bishop of the London Diocese, Most Reverend M.J. Fallon. Their mission was to establish a home to care for women and girls in need. This they did indeed do. Maryvale today is a children's treatment centre serving boys and girls in emotional and mental health crisis. As a result of the Sisters' commitment, the Windsor Essex and Chatham Kent communities have access to a team of mental health experts, including child psychiatrists, psychologists, child and youth specialists, special education teachers, social workers, and art and music therapists.

There were two "branches" to the Good Shepherd Sisters in Windsor: the Apostolic Sisters and the Contemplative Sisters. As the Sisters aged and the number of new recruits in North America dwindled, Sisters across Canada joined their "houses" and, as a result, the Apostolic Sisters left Maryvale in 1988. All of the Canadian Contemplative Sisters joined the Maryvale Convent and lived here until June of 2007, when the six remaining Sisters were moved to the Convent in Toronto.

The last of the Sisters have left Windsor and left Maryvale. They were respected, adored, followed and loved.

It is critical to capture memories and history. This book is an attempt to do just that.

CONNIE MARTIN
EXECUTIVE DIRECTOR

Healing the Hurting

What is Maryvale?

"MARYVALE IS a treatment centre for adolescents and their families where they can receive the support and help they need to reach their fullest potential."…

—Carrie Lee, Program Manager.

What We Are

ASK A dozen people *What is Maryvale?* and you'll probably get six different answers. Anna Piroli Sarkis has heard them all many times during her two decades working at the centre.

"Because it's had such a long history, some people knew it as a place where so-called 'wayward' girls would come for help. That was a different time, a different era. I think some people still see it that way, as a place for kids who have got in trouble, and I really wish we could change that perception. The conflicts we're dealing with are the same kinds of conflicts everyone has in their home, but for some families those are more difficult to manoeuvre through than others. When kids are struggling, when

3

families are struggling, this is a place where people with expertise can help."

Maryvale is situated in the west end of Windsor on seventeen acres of land that once was home to a bona fide sword-carrying British colonel and later was the site of an exclusive country club visited by a bona fide British prince and later still, the place where a few Sisters of the Good Shepherd opened their hearts and their doors to girls who were hurting and had nowhere else to turn.

The Prince Road Convent

The place doesn't look much like a mental-health centre, although the oldest building on campus is pretty imposing. The Convent, an historic property, is two storeys, yellow brick, and looks very much like an institution out of the 1940s, which is when it was built. It served for a quarter-century as a residence and school for the girls and a convent for the Sisters and remained the Sisters' home until the last half dozen of them – elderly and frail – were called in 2007 to The Mother House in Toronto where they'll end their days.

Sister Immaculate Heart near the Chapel

There is a newer addition to the south of The Convent – a three-storey residence attached to an octagonal chapel – and around the corner, off Wells, you'll find the administrative complex – very sixties, one-storey, flat roof, lots of big windows. Beyond the administrative complex there are six raised-ranch "cottages" which is where the kids either live full-time or take part in day programs. The centre offers residential and day-treatment programs for girls and boys between 11 and 18 years of age. It also offers intensive counselling and treatment, and access to a number of psychiatrists, for children who are having mental-health crises.

At any one time there are 75 kids on campus. Very troubled kids. They're all hurting and they've come – or been sent – to Maryvale to heal as best they can.

Maryvale's administrative centre

Billy

A 15-YEAR-OLD boy getting average grades in school, more interested in sports than academics if the truth be told. He was brought by his mom to the emergency room of a local hospital when he began making very strange statements indicating that he could control the world and indeed was responsible for doing so. He had just started claiming that the radio was the key to the portal between heaven and hell.

In looking back on it, he began in grade 8 to have rules regarding how his possessions could and could not be handled. In more recent months his interactions with other students at school were being affected by his obsessive need to keep others away from his things. He had started to make comments to other teens that were not rational and did not make sense.

The parents reported no family history of psychosis.

At the time of admission this boy believed that he could speak directly with God and could control the weather and major natural disasters. He was observed to be mumbling to himself and was having conversations with God.

His parents were extremely distraught and very relieved to have him admitted and seen by the multidisciplinary team. They were devastated and deeply saddened to learn that their son was suffering the first stages of a psychotic illness. It broke their hearts that their child would have to go through such a serious illness. They were very appreciative of any help they could get for their boy.

Deep and Deeper

DR. JANET ORCHARD is the manager of the The Rotary Home for Children and Youth. "The kids who come here have enormous struggles and they don't have the ability to deal with them.

"Most kids will have a reaction to something in their lives but they'll think it through: 'Well, I'd like to do this but that didn't work out' and so on. They can make a plan. They'll include their parents or friends in the discussion. We get kids for whom that process isn't working. So they've got all this pressure happening: peers, family disruptions, academic issues. They jump to a response, kind of a trial and error approach to solving problems in their life, and they'll end up with a bigger problem. At the same time, if there are any other stresses going on at home or school, and as a child you don't feel you can turn to your parents because they have their own stresses, then what the heck are you supposed to do? You just end up shovelling: you dig a hole and you dig it deeper. Then all the other things start happening that makes them more and more isolated from other people. It's all about feeling overwhelmed and inadequate. That's the bottom line.

"There isn't a kid in the world who wants to be here. But a number of them, once they're here, don't want to leave, oddly enough."

Connie Martin is Maryvale's Executive Director. She's to be found in an impossibly cluttered little office in the administrative building: "I really do know where everything is," she'll claim with a laugh, looking at piles of paper and file folders on her

Connie Martin with Sisters

desk, the windowsills, the floor, a table by the wall, a smaller circular desk near the door. She moves papers from two of the chairs at this little table so there's room for us to sit down.

It's been Connie Martin's life's work, for the past quarter century, to support a team of 225 psychiatrists, psychologists, social workers, child-care workers, teachers and therapists whose sole goal is to help these kids get their lives back on the rails. Not an easy thing to do.

"The kids who are here are hurting badly, emotionally or psychologically. It could be temporary or it could be a long-term thing. Some of them could be dealing with a handicap. They are all in incredible distress or they wouldn't be here. That's why we exist. Philosophically, it's not a good thing when kids cannot live with their family. That's not the best. So when that has to happen it tells you they're in terrible distress.

"There's still a shame connected with children having emotional issues, the shame being for the parents thinking it must be a reflection on their parenting, so those parents don't tend to go around talking about it publicly. But we get a lot of kids with wonderful parents. They may not be rich financially but they're rich in family resources. They're committed to one another, they love one another. They can have a child who has a particular temperament, they may be very sensitive to issues in the school, they're being bullied, they're feeling humiliated and they can get themselves so depressed they feel they don't deserve to live, that it's their fault, that there's some deficit in them.

"We also get youngsters who have mental illness starting. It can be terrifying for the youngster who's experiencing it and it can be terrifying for the parents who see their A-level student start to withdraw, grades drop, not wanting to eat. It's our job to diagnose that and to intervene as fast as we can.

"These kids will have a lifelong challenge but what you teach them as teenagers, research now shows, can really improve their lives and alter the severity of the illness. That's where psychiatrists and medication help immensely and why it's been so critical to get psychiatrists to this community. They truly can change kids' lives.

"Some youngsters are really disabled, intellectually very limited with emotional/behavioural issues as well. These kids require a lot of adult supervision. They're very draining on parents. Some are severely autistic.

"Then there are the youngsters who have been abused, neglected, maligned and humiliated and they have been really, really damaged.

"All the psychological theorists would tell you that as you develop emotionally and psychologically there are steps you have to master before you go on to the next step and as you master them you become fully grown and function the way you were intended to function.

"It's just the same as physical development. With kids, it's wired into them to learn to roll over on their own and to want to crawl and then to want to stand up and then to want to walk and teeter around and then to talk. There's a parallel thing emotionally. The first thing kids learn is trust or mistrust of people in the world around them, whether this is a safe place to be or whether it is not a safe place to be, whether it's a comforting place, or not a comforting place.

"Given what they've been exposed to early on, they'll probably never really trust and that'll affect their capacity to hold jobs, to accept the authority of the police officer on the corner or their boss; it'll affect their capacity to maintain a relationship like a marriage, to see their own kids through difficult times, because they've just been too damaged. We do everything we can to modify that, ameliorate it. But these youngsters are really in great distress."

What hope is there for them?

"There's hope they can do better. Everyone here would tell you that 90% of the kids who come here really change. They change because there's a routine that's predictable, there are nurturing adults, they truly feel safe so they can then open themselves up to learning the next few things in life. No kid wants to be out of control. One of our psychologists always says that nobody can feel a sense of self-respect if they know deep inside that they don't know how to control themselves. Kids know that and they don't want to be that way."

Colonel Prince

MARYVALE IS bordered on the west by Prince Road, named for Colonel John Prince who once owned the property. Interesting fellow.

"Colonel Prince was a hale and hearty old country gentleman originating from the country of Hereford and settled under the old regime (The Family Compact) near the town of Sandwich where he farmed his estate and where his family lived."

—from the Sneakers' Site

"A man like Colonel John Prince needs his own (web) page, as opposed to being a footnote in a family history. Prince would be ideal for the silver screen or for a novel. He was bold, intelligent,

Colonel John Prince

Prince Homestead, 1906

(Photos courtesy of Windsor's Community Museum.)

strong, skillful, dangerous and a little bit crazy. He is not a man you want to offend."

—from the Dwyer Laye Family website

Some of those who did offend John Prince wound up dead: summarily shot on The Colonel's orders. More on that in a moment.

Hard to know what The Colonel would have thought of what happened to his estate: forty years after his death (1870) the place became The Essex Golf and Country Club. When the club moved on to a more spacious and more extensively wooded property in 1929, part of Prince's estate became a park (Mic Mac Park, across Prince Road from Maryvale) and the rest was sold to The Sisters of the Good Shepherd.

The Sisters and their homeless and emotionally troubled girls would hardly have been the kind of people who would have found a seat at The Colonel's dining room table, or a warm welcome at the old country club for that matter. By the time the Sisters moved in, The Colonel's old home had been refurbished and enlarged to serve as the clubhouse for the golf course. Still, there were more than a few traces of The Castle, as it became known when The King of the Western District lived there.

The Castle

RECOLLECTIONS OF An Eye Witness:

The old Colonel Prince residence (later the Essex Golf Club) was built in 1822, so it was more than 100 years old when the Sisters took up residence there. There were a lot of spooky little nooks and corners in it, due to poor lighting, with small low windows in several rooms. The ceiling was quite low too, with dark wooden beams. There were at least four fireplaces. There was a secret stairway leading down to a small basement or cellar where some boot-legging is said

12

The original convent, once home to Colonel John Prince, painted by
Sister Gabrielle Dawdy

to have taken place. The upstairs had small rooms with very low ceilings.

The windows were small too. There was a skylight on top of the roof that let in a lot of sun in the summertime – and the summers were a lot hotter and longer then than they are now. The halls downstairs were quite narrow and the rooms were small too, especially the dining room which was rather dark.

It was into this place that the Sisters moved in 1930. As their numbers increased through the years, the place became more and more crowded.

After a long day of toil – caring for the girls, working in the laundry, the kitchen etc, they would retire to their bedrooms in the cold of winter. The engineer usually went home at 7 p.m. so there would be no steam heat during the night or at rising time, which was early. Then they would spend an hour or two in the chapel before breakfast.

It was so chilly you could see your breath. When the heat

did come on – usually at the end of prayer time – the house would get so hot – whew! (There were no thermostats to regulate it.) Then they would spend many a sleepless night in summer battling the heat and mosquitoes that managed to squeeze their way in somehow.

Even though living in the old house did at times impose discomforts, there were compensations. On spring days it was a delight to walk in the garden. The grounds were nicely arranged. Several varieties of flowering bushes and trees were to be seen – lilac, spirea, forsythia, rose of Sharon to name but a few – and flowers and hedges. A large variety of feathered friends were often heard, even if not always seen: wrens, goldfinches, scarlet tanagers, eastern towhees, bluebirds – cardinals and robins, of course. The Sisters found it easy to "walk with God" in the garden as He seemed so near in the beauty of His creation.

The original convent, once home to Colonel John Prince, painted by Sister Gabrielle Dawdy

Shot On The Spot

THE OLD place has certainly been touched by history. Here's the story, as related in *The Windsor Star*:

It was in the old house that Colonel Prince and his friend Doctor Hume, were eating breakfast (one December morning in 1838) when a messenger arrived at the house reporting 150 "Patriots" were marching on Windsor. The Colonel, dressed in hunting attire, buckled on his sword and rode off to raise his troops. The doctor went looking for wounded.

The invaders wanted to make Upper and Lower Canada a republic. They fled after 21 men were killed by militia volleys. After the rout, Colonel Prince met the doctor for the second time that day. His body was being eaten by hogs in a pig pen. One arm had been hacked off with an axe and a bayonet had been thrust through Doctor Hume's chest.

The militia commander ordered four Patriot prisoners shot on the spot. He classed the invaders as pirates and as such liable for execution without trial. When critics of the colonel's execution demanded an answer The Colonel gave a characteristically blunt reply: "I ordered them to be shot and it was done accordingly."

Since The Colonel took up his 200 acres in Sandwich, rambling additions have been attached to the original square structure. The house was part of history during the 27-year period when Colonel Prince was its occupant. At the height of his popularity after the twin rebellions of 1837-8 had been put down he was referred to in the press as "king of the western district, if not Upper Canada".

The Ghosts

"THIS PLACE is so rich in history," says Connie Martin. "I find it fascinating that on this earth we're walking on, and probably right where we're sitting ... someone with the personality right out of a book like Colonel Prince would have walked here. And just think of people whose lives have been lived on these grounds, how people lived their lives, the different eras.

"Colonel Prince was a larger than life character, given how he could just order people to be shot. He didn't even know who they were, if they were good people or bad people, that didn't matter.

"Then you transition to people playing golf here. I noticed that Wallace Stewart was mentioned (as a member of the Essex Golf Club). Wally Stewart was an elderly gentleman in Rotary, a real gentleman, the old-English kind of gentleman – I respected him immensely – and I never knew he would have been on these grounds playing golf.

"You think of the Sisters and that was another era. You think of all the ladies in town who would come to their aid and would put on the teas to support them. What kind of an era was that? It's just so interesting."

Lots of ghosts: some with swords and guns, some with golf clubs and caddies.

1910 – The Golf Club

FROM *A History of Essex Golf and Country Club* , by Jeff Mingay (2002):

When the Oak Ridge Golf Club purchased the Prince Farm in 1910, Club directors attempted to preserve the character of Colonel Prince's old farmhouse while converting it into a proper golf clubhouse.

For example, the Colonel's old wainscoted dining room was intelligently left intact. There, over the fireplace, hung a crayon portrait of Colonel Prince himself. This portrait served as a fitting reminder to all Essex members of the Prince Farm's historic roots.

The new Essex course opened for play on the Prince Farm in the spring of 1912.

Ghosts of old soldiers, ghosts of old golfers, ghosts of old nuns: it's hard not to bump into them when you're wandering around campus. Particularly the Sisters who were still living their cloistered lives in the old convent as recently as 2007. Their absence has been felt. Their presence still is.

A Huge Void

MARILYN MORRISON and Connie Doyle are long-time members of The Associates, a group which volunteered to help the Sisters in any number of ways: from running bake sales to running errands. They remember very well the day the nuns left Maryvale.

"It was so moving," says Marilyn. "So sad. That whole week was just full of tears."

"It was such a huge void," says Connie.

"We felt such a devotion to them," says Marilyn. "They were just so genuine, and so full of love. They exemplified what we're here for, what our role as Christians is: to love our neighbours as ourselves."

The Nuns

"THEY SYMBOLIZED something that I think all of us deep inside either do believe or want to believe exists," says Connie Martin, "which is a higher power and that there's something bigger than all of us that we can count on. They symbolized a way of life where you make a commitment to something and you literally give your whole life to it and that's so unlike most of us. They made this incredible commitment and gave forty or sixty years of their life to it.

"The Order was set up years ago to protect women and children. I'm told it was one of the first Catholic orders of nuns who were progressive enough to devote themselves to the causes of women. The females they took care of were homeless – they had been abandoned or orphaned. Often in those days, too, way back

Final profession, July 22, 1950:
Sister Agnes, Sister Veronica, Sister Blanche, Sister Helena,
Sister Ethel, Sister Dorothea

when, they talked about getting disabled children. Some families would leave a child on the doorstep. As society evolved there wasn't such a need for orphanages, so they started to work with women and girls who were in emotional need."

When the Sisters first opened their home in Windsor there was no social safety net and there were no government cheques to pay for such services. How did a group of nuns, who took vows of poverty, manage to pay the bills down through the years?

"They will tell you that manna just came from heaven, that they would trust that they would get what they needed and then it would be there. They talked about how the community of Windsor came forward with things to make it work. But they were frugal." They saved their nickels and pennies; they approached everyone they could to make donations – some of them pretty substantial.

The Sisters started Maryvale as a vocational school for girls: hoping to prepare them for useful and successful lives. The schooling had to do, mostly, with things like cooking and sewing, typing and shorthand. Practical subjects that would at that time serve the girls well: help them find jobs and husbands.

Over the years, Maryvale was transformed from a privately-funded school for girls into a full-fledged mental health treatment centre, funded in part by the province, in part by private donations, and it now serves girls and boys. The youngsters are to be found in several cottages which stand where The Colonel's Castle once stood surrounded by orchards and gardens and farm fields.

The Treatment

MARYVALE IS at the cutting edge of treatment for children who are having mental health crises. Maryvale and Windsor Regional Hospital recently received a "Best of the Best" award from the Ontario Hospitals Association for an innovative program which features hospital beds located on Maryvale's campus.

"We have the first, and probably still the only, program in the province where we have mental health hospital beds for children and teens off the hospital site," says Connie Martin.

Janet Orchard is the manager of the hospital bed program and one of the psychologists who treats the youngsters who come to the Rotary Home for Children and Youth. "We see boys and girls as young as 8 and as old as 18 who come either to the hospital in a mental-health crisis or to one of the psychiatrists in the community.

"You're looking at kids who are experiencing the onset of a significant depression: they may have attempted suicide; or they may be experiencing the onset of a first-episode psychosis or severe anxiety disorder. We also get kids who are in the midst of a situational crisis where a lot of things come together and they lack the coping skills to deal with them and they may act out by injuring themselves."

When Janet Orchard speaks of "depression", she's not speaking of kids feeling a little down in the dumps. "When you're talking about a major depressive disorder, you're talking about a level of depression that includes no capacity to experience pleasure.

"Kids who are experiencing normal mood swings appear glum but if they're on the phone with their friends, or out with their friends, they can look pretty happy. Someone who's experiencing a major depressive disorder will withdraw from normal social activity. They lack energy. They stop going to school, they stop doing their normal pleasurable activities, they are extremely negative and pessimistic."

What's going on with the kids who attempt suicide?

"They may be, and usually are, experiencing disruption in their peer relationships which are, of course, so crucial to kids and so they're feeling isolated and alone. Often there are stresses in the family or it may be a death in the family: 'I've lost someone I was super close to so not only have I got these other things happening now, someone I would normally have gone to is not available to me'.

"The youngsters come to one of the local ERs, the pediatric crisis team is paged, they go in, do the assessment, if they think an admission is necessary, the child will be admitted. They're certainly working very hard to divert kids from hospital. They see about 400 kids a year in the ER and of those we get about 190.

"The admission is usually made for safety reasons. If the social worker is getting a feeling the child's safety is of concern, has any squeamishness at all, then the psychiatrist will admit. Similarly, if the psychiatrist is hearing that this is a kid who is presenting with significant depression, they will automatically admit.

"So in they come (to Maryvale). The purpose of the program is to do assessment and stabilization of crisis. The average length of stay is only about eight days, so we have to move pretty fast. There will be meetings with the child and the parents. We do an evaluation of the need or absence of need for any medical treatment.

"There will be a psychological assessment. Sometimes the doctor will ask that we record the child's moods throughout the day. She might also want us to track the child's activity levels. That information helps the doctor with the diagnosis, and judging whether the medication is working.

"The day includes school and recreation activities and art and music therapy, so we get a lot of opportunities to observe and to coach coping skills. The kids always say they need to learn how to manage things differently. They're not using that language but the bottom line is: 'well, that didn't work out all that well so I better learn another way of handling this.' That becomes our focus, the whole way through."

Some of the kids who leave the Rotary home end up staying in one of Maryvale's other cottages for more extensive treatment. The rest head back home with Maryvale and Regional Children's Centre organizing individual therapy for the youngster.

"They know they're going to meet that person two or three days after discharge. So then they can leave knowing there's something there for them. They don't have to worry that after this intense level of service here there's nothing there for them because that can be such a danger zone for the child and the parents."

That's the hospital program. Broadly speaking, there are two other types of programs at Maryvale: day treatment and residential treatment. "A small number of students live here," says Connie Martin. "Those are usually kids with extremely difficult problems and some of them don't have families. When there's a sense that they've stabilized, when they're doing better, we try to get them a more normal place to live.

"Most of the kids come here during the day. They go to their own homes overnight. The Greater Essex County District School Board provides us with special education teachers. So there's full-fledged schooling. Those cottages also provide after-school programming for another set of kids who attend community schools during the day but are very challenging kids.

"In order to help support families and help parents keep normal jobs those kids would come to us right after school and stay until 7 or 8 at night, have supper, play games, that sort of thing. If you've got a really challenging child, that can help keep your family together. The rest of the family can come home from work and settle down, have supper with their other children before this one who requires incredible supervision comes home.

"The treatment is really a combination of things. Probably the most important thing for the kids is that their day is so nurturing, so predictable, so clear about where the limits are and staff are so consistent with them that you can just see them settle. It's like balloons when the air starts coming out of them. They come in so escalated and they just settle. Whenever we are evaluated, which happens frequently when you run a residential program, the kids are interviewed privately and every single time the evaluators will come out saying that what really impressed them is that the kids say how much they like the staff, how safe they feel with the staff.

"Helping the child to feel safe is our first priority. Safe emotionally. Safe that they're okay. They feel that they're out of control, and maybe their family is out of control, they're scared, they know something is going on with themselves although they don't know what it is. So it's important to have them settle, to feel that they'll be all right here. That's what the staff do. And that in itself is immense treatment for a lot of these kids.

"Then there are all kinds of other layers.

"The psychologists will meet with them and do assessments. Often we find kids who have incredible learning disabilities. They don't process information accurately and they don't read social situations accurately. They don't read your cues. They've been misinterpreted as being defiant. They're not defiant. They just can't figure out what you're messaging to them. That happens a lot. Psychologists will do an assessment and find out they've got these learning disabilities. The psychiatrists will see them and determine if some medication would help. So there are all kinds of layers."

The School

MARYVALE PUTS a very high premium on education. All the children who come here attend school, at least for part of the day.

The school – ten bright and well-lit classrooms whose windows look out on the park-like campus – is attached to the back of the administration building.

In a narrow little office situated between two classrooms, you'll find manager Janet Glos.

"Many kids have lots of special needs. Seldom do we get a youngster who doesn't have a learning disability so we're always adapting and working at what's the best way for this child to learn.

"Our kids have usually had years where they were not successful in school, did not have good report cards, did not fit in. So when they get here we're dealing with a real history of resistance to work and lots of self-esteem issues. Kids have to feel comfortable and understood and that takes a lot of energy."

1919 – The Royal Visit

FROM *A History of Essex Golf and Country Club* , by Jeff Mingay (2002):

On October 23, 1919, Edward, Prince of Wales visited Windsor on a cross-country tour of Canada. That evening "one hundred and twenty-five prominent residents of the Border Cities" toasted the Prince during a banquet held at the Essex Golf and Country Club in his honour.

The Prince arrived at the club on an Essex Terminal passenger train. He was then transported by automobile across the fourth fairway to the clubhouse. Among the guests in attendance were Detroit industrialists Henry Ford and Essex club president Gordon M. McGregor, who gave the official toast.

The Staff

THERE ARE two doors leading to Connie Martin's office – one leading in from the front office area, the other leading in from an interior corridor. Both are usually open and people seem to have a habit of walking right in – like the manager standing in front of Connie's desk making a point about something. The manager finishes making her point and heads out one door and I enter through the other.

I've come to ask about the staff: "Tell me about the kind of people who work here."

"You have to like psychology. You have to wonder what makes people tick and you have to want to help kids. It's very, very hard work for no other reason than we have to constantly regulate ourselves emotionally. We're a mental health treatment centre. If we can't have the best mental health around these kids, then we have no business working with them at all.

"A lot of people grow into this work. People will tell you that they've learned so much about themselves. They wouldn't want to work anywhere else now. But if you're here, you have to look at yourself. The conversation you just walked in on was one of those conversations. The manager is annoyed about my approach to a problem we've been dealing with. Well, that's exactly the kind of conversation that has to take place. So I have to sit with that and think 'okay, what am I going to do differently?' And, yes, something will happen.

"That's why it's such tough work, because in most places, people wouldn't be bothered with that. You can't let something fester. We're not going to be what we want to be if we do that. In three months, it would disintegrate if we didn't force ourselves to face these issues. You learn to be honest with one another."

Living a Dream

SANDY TOMKINS has been connected with Maryvale since the 1960s, when her mother volunteered to help at fund-raising bazaars, and has worked at Maryvale for more than 30 years. "It was always my dream to work here and have some sort of an impact on children. Not everyone gets to fulfill their dreams.

"Every now and then I'll bump into someone I worked with here 20 or 30 years ago and they'll say 'Oh my goodness, do you remember me?' That just happened to me recently and as soon as she walked away I remembered her.

"It's nice.

"I think I do have an impact on the kids. I don't see them that much anymore. I'm on the midnight shift. So I see them if they get sick, or if they get up in the night. I'm here in the morning when they get up. They look forward to us coming in and doing special things with them. I make home-made soups for them, or muffins, or cookies, whatever. It's kind of a grandmotherly, comforting kind of relationship."

1920s – The Golf Course

FROM *A History of Essex Golf and Country Club* , by Jeff Mingay (2002):

Unfortunately, very few photographs of the Prince Farm course have been located. And its exact layout is a distant, incoherent memory.

Long-time Essex member W. Wallace Stuart remembered the course as being relatively hilly. Curiously, Stuart and his brother, Essex past-president John J. Stuart, played the Prince Farm course with their mother and father on the last day it was used by the club before being handed over to the Great Lakes Land Company for residential development in 1929. The following day, the Stuart brothers played the new Matchette Road course on its first day opened for play.

The Toughest Part

WHAT'S THE toughest part of working with these upset kids?

Lisa, a supervisor, has a pretty good take on that. You'll find her in Maryvale's assessment and receiving program – the place where many of the kids make their first stop after coming in for treatment.

As you might imagine, the kids aren't in the best of shape and they're not always in the most pleasant frame of mind. "As a youth worker, you may be the target as the youngster deals with the issues they're going through. You have to let all that go. We have our own emotions, our own feelings. But you quickly learn not to take things personally.

"It's not easy. We're all human. So you have to have that outlet with one another and be able to vent if you're frustrated and angry. But do it outside." She laughs. "We still hold the kids accountable. Some of these behaviours are quite significant and the kids have to be removed from the group. But afterward, we see what might have led them to do that: 'What happened here, what were your triggers, why do you think this happened? How will you take responsibility for it?'"

1928 – The Great Depression

FROM *A History of Essex Golf and Country Club* , by Jeff Mingay (2002):

In August 1928, with a new 18-hole golf course and clubhouse under construction on Matchette Road in the Town of LaSalle, Essex directors agreed to sell the Prince Farm to the Great Lakes Land Company, Inc. of Detroit for $300,000. Eighty thousand dollars was paid in cash. And, with a bond issue of $44,000 against the property, the remaining $220,000 was to be paid in six equal installments of $36,666 beginning in 1930.

Under the tutelage of company president Edward E.

Beals, the Great Lakes Land Company planned to subdivide Prince Farm course into a prestigious residential development called Old Essex. However, shortly after their acquisition of the property, the Great Depression had a severe impact on the company's financial position and the development was placed on hold. By 1931, the Great Lakes Land Company had defaulted on three scheduled payments due to the club.

The Prince Farm was not disposed of until 1932 when Essex directors executed a deed transferring the remaining portions of the property to "Beals Old Essex Realty Ltd.". Still, the fanciful plans for an Old Essex neighbourhood never materialized.

Saving Souls

CARRIE LEE's office is not the easiest one to find. It may well be the quietest. It's up on the top floor of the old Convent, with a window looking out on Prince Road and the baseball diamonds of Mic Mac Park. To get to her office, you have to come in a ground-floor door, then ascend three echoey flights of stairs, go down the terrazzo hall and make a left. Quite an office. She even has her own bathroom.

She smiles: "I think this was the Mother Superior's bedroom. She got her own bathroom and she was able to look out the door and keep an eye on everyone." "Everyone" being the nuns whose quarters were considerably less luxurious: single cot, single bedside table in a cubicle whose walls are like office dividers and whose doors are curtains.

Those Sisters are much on Carrie's mind since they moved out. "I think we have to keep telling people about the history of the Sisters because otherwise that's the piece that will get lost over time."

Carrie is one of the senior staff who takes part in staff training and orientation. "I talk about the history, I'm able to talk about Saint Mary Euphrasia who began all this, and how the Order has grown until now it's all over the world. Mary Euphrasia was a woman way beyond her years in terms of her knowledge and the connections she made. Back then she had to take a buggy to get from one place to another and it would take her days but she would get there and get what she wanted. It was always all about saving children's souls. And we still do that work here."

Working with Sister Pauline

WHEN SANDY TOMKINS started at Maryvale in April of 1976, the Sisters were still working in the cottages. "I was hired by the Sisters. I worked with Sister Emily in Cottage 4.

"Sister Pauline was the supervisor there. She was very strict. We used to write logs on the children. We did long-form back then. Some people would get right to the point but others would write and write and write, they'd write pages. You would come in on your shift and you were expected to read all this information on the children and know exactly what happened on that shift because if Sister Pauline came and you didn't know what had happened, you were in hot water. She was just like a sergeant. She would question you on the shift the day before. It was a little intimidating. You had better know what you were supposed to know."

1929 – Arrival of the Nuns in Windsor

FROM *A Book of Remembrance, Fifty years of loving labour for the glory of God and the good of mankind 1929 – June 3rd – 1979*:

Five nuns arrived in Windsor June 3, 1929. Mother Mary of St. Alphonsus with Sisters Mary of St. Juliana, Sister Immaculate Heart, Sister St. Gerard and Sister Incarnation. We took up temporary residence in a duplex at 9 McEwan Avenue in the Parish of Holy Name of Mary.

On June 21, the first girl was received into residential

care. Soon girls began to arrive. Lovely girls whom we were glad to help. There were ten in all. They occupied the top flat. The need for a larger place became urgent. We went house hunting.

Mr. Beals of the Great Lakes Land Company held 81 acres which featured the old Prince home, surrounded by beautiful gardens and trees, and two other buildings, at the corner of Prince Road and College Avenue. The four acres on which these buildings were located were valued at $81,000. This was the location we set our eyes and hearts on.

Our board managed to obtain the property for us for only $45,000 on June 30, 1930. Of course, we had no money, so the Bishop loaned us $50,000 at 6% payable every six months and – the Lord be praised – we paid it with the kind help of the people of Windsor. So with hearts full of joy and gratitude to God and Mr. Beals we moved from our cramped quarters on McEwan Avenue to our present location on July 1, 1930.

On seeing the house and grounds in such good condition, we were inspired to call it "Windsor Castle", a name that stuck through the years until its dilapidated condition made the name a joke.

The old Essex Golf Club, semi-furnished, became the Convent and Chapel, the second building which had been the men's locker room was used as a dorm for the girls and half of the third building was set aside for the girls' use. The other half was outfitted as a laundry. Later we bought more property and we now have 17 acres.

A Safe Place

As CONNIE MARTIN says: "Helping the child to feel safe is our first priority."

How do you do that?

"There are two components," says Janet Glos, manager in

Maryvale's school. "There's the treatment skill component: knowing how to handle them, how to talk to them, knowing how much structure they need, how much support they need. You're coming up with a unique plan for each kid: what are their educational needs, what are their treatment needs, and then putting that in place.

"The other component is making sure … that I'm listening to the staff, I'm hearing their frustrations, solving problems quickly and alleviating their stress. If the staff doesn't feel supported, that affects everything we do in terms of the treatment. If all that is in place, then they can be patient with the kids and they can do their jobs. It's always working to make it all come together."

1930 – Early Days

SPEAKING OF ghosts, Here are "Recollections of one of the girls" from *A Book of Remembrance, Fifty years of loving labour for the glory of God and the good of mankind 1929 – June 3rd – 1979:*

When the Sisters moved from McEwan Avenue to their new location (the Essex Golf Club) there were only five of us (girls). With the Sisters we shared the excitement, hopes, fears, uncertainties, work and the inevitable poverty that goes with pioneering, but kind benefactors soon came to our aid.

Mrs. LePain supplied us with bread for two years. Dr. Denise sent us lots of cantaloupe. Norton-Palmer (then a flourishing hotel) supplied for years our Christmas dinner, already cooked, all because Mother St. Alphonsus once said to Mr. Norton "God Bless You!" Miss Lyons sent us a cake every Tuesday in honour of St. Anthony. Through the sisters we received medical and dental care gratis from kindly doctors. Namely: Drs. E. Beuglet, E.C. Young, R.J. Coyle. L.J. Girard, C.V. Hinsperger. B.A. Ballard and others.

Besides enjoying our own home-made fun, the Knights of Columbus came often to entertain us, as well as Assump-

The Property as it looked in the 1930s

tion Choir and Mrs. Clare Rivard, who sang for us and also gave us singing lessons free.

Laundry work was started shortly after we got settled in our new home. Assumption College, as it was then called (the high school was built later) set the tumblers rolling by sending in hundreds of blankets to be laundered. We really enjoyed the work and "blessed" the hours with hymns and prayers. New girls coming in would soon catch the spirit and the tunes and join in, singing lustily.

During the nice days of spring and summer we would sit out under the old oak tree and Sister Immaculate Heart would hold her daily catechism class.

We recall with affection and gratitude all that the dear Sisters did for us. The beautiful example of self-forgetfulness, love and care they displayed, making all kinds of sacrifices so that we could have the best. They did all they could to help us in every way and we were really happy, contented and grateful.

The old Prince Home, later a golf clubhouse, finally a convent

1934 – Visit of the Cardinal

FROM *The Windsor Star*, June 11, 1934:

Cardinal Villeneuve bade farewell to the Border Cities yesterday afternoon, taking with him the memory of a spontaneous welcome during his brief stay here and leaving with clergy and laity regrets that he could not have prolonged his visit. Departure of His Eminence followed excursions to the Monastery of the Good Shepherd in Sandwich, Hotel Dieu and St. Anne's Church, Tecumseh.

At the Monastery of the Good Shepherd, Cardinal Villeneuve said: "My dear children, there should be no place that would give me greater pleasure to visit than here."

Sister Humour

IF THE SISTERS gave out honourary memberships, Olga Howchuk would certainly have had one. She has spent countless hours over the last 30 years helping out at the Convent: she's helped

Sister Bernadette Gauer, Sister Gabrielle Dawdy, Olga Howchuk

in the convent gift shop; she's baked everything you can imagine for bake sales and bazaars from the 70s right through to today.

How did all this begin?

"I had a friend who was in hospital and she had two nuns come to visit her. One was Sister Mary Theresa Caron. I told her I lived right around the corner from the convent and she said why don't you come and visit us and that's how it started. This was in the 70s and I started visiting her on Sunday afternoons."

She was taken with the Sisters from that very first encounter. "They make such an impression on you. It was the friendliness they showed you. They made you feel welcome at any time. In happy times and in sorrow, they're there for you."

For the next few minutes she goes through the names of some of the Sisters she has known down through the years: "Sister Francis was the superior, Sister Mary Elizabeth, Sister Mary Breen. Sister Mary Breen was very Irish and she was just a sweetheart. I would visit her and I have beautiful things that she gave me." Interesting she should mention this because as anyone who knew the nuns will tell you, though they had very little, they were generous to a fault. An example: one day Olga was helping Sister Veronica in the gift shop at the convent. She remarked on a vase that she admired. "It was a beautiful vase, I believe it was cornflower, and she said 'Would you like to have it' so she gave it to me, of course with permission from Sister Bernadette. I still have it. I have beautiful flowers in it."

As a regular visitor to the convent, Olga had some glimpses of life behind the walls. "They're like your own family. They have their likes and their dislikes. They like their sweets like we all do. And when their birthdays come they still expect something. And when they do get a gift they are so appreciative, even if it's a small little thing, they know it comes from love. They do have their fun times. They had their dances. They would dance around in the community room.

"They were down to earth. They had their moments. You could tell when somebody was a little angry but they didn't show it, they didn't come out with unkind words."

No yelling?

"No yelling. At least they didn't yell when I was there." And she laughs, at the preposterous thought.

What impact did the Sisters have at Maryvale?

"I have never come across anyone who hasn't been impressed by the Sisters and 'felt their warmth. Even though there was a crowd around you, they made you feel as though you were the only one in the room."

What did they mean to the kids?

"The day they left, my husband and I came down, and all the kids were lined up when the van was leaving. There must have been everyone from Maryvale there to say goodbye to them. I feel their impact was the greatest."

Olga opens the manila envelope she brought with her. Inside, a calendar and a sheaf of paper. Sister Gabrielle is the one who did the calendar. It's a lovely calendar, featuring some of Sister Gabrielle's watercolours depicting the old Prince residence, the McIsaac residence, and the chapel.

There are also photographs of the nuns working with children

Sisters dancing

in the classroom, nuns sitting in the chapel posing for one last group shot (there are 26 of them, so this photo must have been taken quite a while ago) and there are other snapshots showing the nuns on an outing at a beach, nuns with their volunteer friends (there's even one of Olga with Sisters).

The sheaf of papers, as it turns out, is a collection of jokes compiled by Sister Irene. "At first I thought she looked kind of stern but I got to know her and she's the one who gave me all these funny little stories."

Herewith, a sampler from Sister Irene's Joke Book:

Word definitions:
Bowel: a letter like A.E.I.O.U.
Fibula: a small lie
Impotent: famous, well known

The following comes from a Catholic elementary school test.

Kids were asked questions about the Old and New Testaments. These are their answers, word for word.

—Moses led the Jews to the Red Sea where they made unleavened bread which is bread without any ingredients.

—The Egyptians were all drowned in the dessert. Afterwards, Moses went up to Mount Cyanide to get the ten commanments.

—Solomon, one of David's sons, had 300 wives and 700 porcupines.

—The first commandments was when Eve told Adam to eat the apple.

—The epistles were the wives of the apostles.

1940 – The Good Shepherd Auxiliary

FROM *A Book of Remembrance, Fifty years of loving labour for the glory of God and the good of mankind 1929 – June 3rd – 1979:*

In the spring of 1940, a Ladies Auxiliary was initiated whose purpose was to sponsor social events such as teas, bridge parties and bazaars etc. These events brought us the financial assistance necessary to carry on our apostolate.

Something Special

ANYONE WHO worked at Maryvale when the Sisters were still around will have a lot of fond memories of all the nuns. Sandy Tomkins especially remembers Sister Anne Marie. "She was so warm and friendly and outgoing and the kids loved her. They could be angry at her, but they still had a lot of respect for her.

"Sister Emily taught those kids how to crochet and make slippers and mittens. We would get donations of left-over material and we would cut them into squares and we and the girls made home-made quilts. Sister Emily started that, home-made quilts for the families for Christmas. To this day I still have mine.

"Sister Anne Marie was the last one to work on the floor with the kids. That would have been in the late 70s."

1940 – The Villa

FROM *A Book of Remembrance, Fifty years of loving labour for the glory of God and the good of mankind 1929 – June 3rd – 1979:*

In 1940, a split-level cottage was built for the girls to relieve cramped quarters, serving as a dormitory upstairs and a kitchen and dining room downstairs. It was officially opened on Dec. 8th of the same year.

The girls were just thrilled with their new quarters and took special pride in keeping them clean and sparkling.

When they moved into the large brick building called "Maryvale" erected in 1948-49, this place was used successively by various groups on campus and it now serves as a guest house for the Sisters' relatives and friends. It is now known as the "Villa".

A Million Stories

SANDY TOMKINS often finds herself thinking of some of the hundreds of youngsters she has worked with during her 30 years at Maryvale.

"I could tell you a million stories.

"There were just so many. I'd love to know whatever happened to a lot of kids that I worked with. I know you can't but it would be nice to know."

Sometimes, though, it's not nice to know.

"There are some who have had such extremely difficult backgrounds, you wonder how they ever survived. I found the obituary of a young girl we had here a few years ago who committed suicide. I'd gone to her funeral. She was a tough one. But she was such a sweet girl. She wanted to kill herself, ongoingly, all the time. She finally succeeded. There are so many troubled children. It just makes you sad when you think about it. You wish there weren't so many."

A Safe Place

CARRIE LEE has a pretty good perspective when it comes to seeing the shape the kids are in when they first arrive at Maryvale. A lot of the kids are hurting. Emotionally. Psychologically. Sometimes physically. It has to be heart-breaking to see them.

Carrie pauses for several seconds before responding. "Hmm," she finally says. And then, after another few seconds' pause, "There are a lot of those kids. And this is what makes me think of the Sisters. They always talked about healing souls. You see kids who come through here and they're so broken up. To watch the process of healing is absolutely amazing. It makes me emotional just thinking about it. They just blossom, even the most damaged, damaged kids. It's fascinating to watch that process."

It's paramount that the kids feel – in some cases for the first time in their lives – they're out of harm's way. "There are things we do and you can say this is why they feel safe. But there's also just a feeling here. You walk on these grounds and there's a feeling here. There are places where you just feel better and safer and more comfortable, and I guess for the kids it's that feeling of immediately connecting with the staff who are so gifted in terms of being able to connect with kids so rapidly. You're always going to be respected, you're always going to be heard and I think that's what kids feel when they come here."

Children Cherished

From *A Book of Remembrance, Fifty years of loving labour for the glory of God and the good of mankind 1929 – June 3rd – 1979.* Sister M. Teresa Davies (Maryvale 1946-51).

June 16, 1946 inaugurated my stay in Windsor. Father Guinan CSB officiated at the ceremony of installation. Next day a tornado made an indelible impression and that, along with the appearance of "Windsor Castle" convinced me that I had arrived at the last place God made. However, June in The Sun Parlour of Canada brought lovely days and "Windsor Castle" draped in Wisteria and Trumpet vines became a thing of beauty in spite of broken stucco and leaky roof.

What impressed me most was the beautiful spirit of charity and poverty in the little group of Sisters and the lovely family atmosphere amongst the girls, who looked like children really cherished.

Doing Laps

There were two orders of Sisters at Maryvale: one order worked directly with the children in the cottages; the other was a contemplative order. The Sisters of that order lived in the convent and never left it. They wouldn't even go out for a walk on campus. That changed in 2001. "With the whole-hearted approval of higher religious authorities the Contemplative Sisters begin walking the grounds. The blessings obtained were mutual."

Sandy Tomkins would second that: "The Sisters always had an impact. The Sisters walked around campus and the kids could see them all the time. The Sisters were always just such a big part of our environment whether they were on campus with the kids or not.

"The kids would ask if the Sisters would come and visit them and at Christmas time, and at special times – holidays – they did.

40

Sister Anne Jessome, the Joker

The kids really liked that and they looked forward to it. They had a lot of feelings toward them.

"I'm sad that they're gone."

Of Squirrels and Toilets

Frank Chauvin has a lot of special memories of many of the Sisters. Sister Anne particularly. "She'd feed the damned squirrels and they were getting into the attic and the other nuns were complaining that the squirrels were running around in the attic. I said 'Anne, you've got to quit feeding those squirrels' and she said 'They're God's animals and I must feed them.' I said, 'There are squirrels all over the place.' And she said 'Oh, I just give them a little bit of food.'

"Anyway, one day I was just getting ready to leave, must have been around 11:30 and I hear 'Mr. Chauvin!' and it was Sister Anne. She said the toilet on the second floor wasn't shutting off and it was making noise all the time. So we went up there. I said, 'Anne, you go in there first,' because a couple of times I'd be in there fixing a toilet in one stall when one of the nuns would come in to the next stall and then I can't leave until she leaves and she don't know I'm in the stall beside her and I'm waiting and waiting. So I said 'Anne, you stand guard at the door.'

"So I go in there and it's just the ball that has to be adjusted. But as I was bending the arm, I broke it and now I can't shut it off. So I said, 'Anne, come here. Sit on the toilet here. And hold this (the arm) and don't let go because there'll be water all over the place'. She said 'Where are you going?' and I said 'I'm going for lunch' and she said 'You can't leave me here.' So I was heading off to the hardware store but then I ran into Sister Virginia. I said 'Have you got a camera?' and she said 'Yes,' and I said 'Well, go up to the second floor bathroom, the second stall, open the door and you'll get a good picture.' And she did. And she got a great picture.

"So these were some of the comical things that happened. It was just a joy to go there. They were always glad to see me because, like I said, they'd been confined to that place for years and never had a chance to let loose. They had a sense of humour. They'd love it when I teased them and they'd feed me ammunition to tease the other sisters. I had a lot of fun with them. They were special. Those were good years."

Obstacles

"THE OBSTACLES we face in kids' lives are things that are outside their control and outside our control," says Janet Glos. "Some of the kids have so many things going on in their lives, especially the kids who have been removed from their families. It's an emotional roller-coaster and it can't always be resolved in a year, or a year and a half.

"I saw one little guy yesterday who's been removed from his

home. There was a plan for him to go home, he had all kinds of hope, he had all his stuff packed, then it was decided that other things need to happen before he can go back.

"From that moment, he lost his hope, he's frustrated, he's angry and he's gone right back in terms of his behaviour to where he was before. He'd packed up his stuff I don't know how many times. It's heartbreaking for staff, it's frustrating. And you have to change your goals with him. He isn't going to change his day-to-day behaviours and make all these gains in the classroom emotionally and behaviourally because all this other stuff is going on. So your goal changes and our job becomes just supporting him, just being there for a kid who's going through an horrific time.

"You let him know you're on his side, you're there for him. You talk to him about how he feels about things, you help him express his anger, sometimes at his parents, sometimes at us, sometimes just generally. You're also helping him deal with how he's thinking about it. You're gently trying to help him look at it in a different way: 'What would happen if you did go home and your Dad wasn't able to care for you? What was that like in the past when your Dad wasn't able to care for you?' You try to help him think about it differently. We tell him: 'It isn't that you're not a good kid, it's isn't that they don't love you, this isn't a reflection on you.' You challenge them to re-frame the situation and that changes the way in which they cope with it and feel about it."

Charming In A Pearl Grey Frock

FROM *The Windsor Star*, May 1, 1949:

What started as a dream 20 years ago when the Sisters of the Good Shepherd first came to Windsor from Toronto became a reality yesterday as Mayor Arthur J. Reaume cut the ribbon that officially opened Maryvale Vocational Training School on Prince Road, assisted by Rev. Sister Mary St. Theresa, Mother Superior.

The new two-storey building is the first one especially

Prince Road convent under construction, 1949 (front)

Rear of Prince Road convent completed

Discuss Plans for Good Shepherd Auxiliary Tea

Discussing last-minute plans for the annual tea of the Good Shepherd Auxiliary, to be staged tomorrow afternoon, from 1 until 6 o'clock, at Maryvale, on Prince road, are, left to right, Mother St. Ambrose, Mrs. Joseph A. Conway, auxiliary president, and Sister Mary Immaculate Heart. Proceeds from tomorrow's affair will go toward the building fund for the convent to be erected, it is hoped, in the near future, as the present convent, which is the old Essex Golf Club, is in bad disrepair.

(Star Staff Photo.)

designed for the work being carried on by the sisters and it is an impressive one. The rooms are bright and airy and in their delicate pastel shades have a most cheerful look. A large crowd of interested friends of the [Good Shepherd] auxiliary and the sisters turned out to inspect the new building and enjoy tea which was served from an attractive table in the dining room.

Receiving the guests throughout the afternoon and evening with the Mother Superior were the Rev. Sister Mary Immaculate Heart, Mrs. Gabriel J. Boutette, president of the auxiliary, charming in a pearl grey frock, styled with a draped square neckline and a pink straw cloth hat trimmed with flowers and veiling, Mrs. J.A. Conway, wearing a grey suit and white straw sailor [hat], trimmed with blue ribbon.

Hostess convenors were Mrs. Charles Parsons, wearing a navy dress and a red hat and ...

Pouring tea throughout the afternoon were ...

The Associates

THE LADIES, charming in their pearl grey frocks, are long gone. But for the last two decades, another group of ladies has stepped in to fill that void. They're known as The Associates. Marilyn Morrison is the leader of the group which, though the Sisters are gone, still does what it can to keep the spirit of the Sisters alive.

"The Associates is a group of women that was started in 1991 by Sister Joan Marie Looby. I'm the designated leader. I haven't been voted in or anything, but that's my role. Our purpose is to bring the mission and the charisma of the Sisters to the people. It's part of our vows to assist the Sisters in their daily work and in their prayers. Many of us drove them around to appointments, we brought meals in for them, anything we could do to help.

"We had monthly meetings with Sister Grace and as she aged, they got funnier and funnier because she might fall asleep while she chaired the meeting, or she might forget what we were talking about or planning. But we just loved getting together with them. Sister Grace was our chair and when she passed away Sister Gabrielle took over.

"We're doing what we can now that the Sisters are gone. We can't do any charity work for them but our mission now is to carry on the Sisters' role at Maryvale, to help the children as best we can. We just had a bake sale and we had a book sale in December. We're planning to build a memorial garden on the site and part of our fund-raising is for that. We are involved to some degree with the staff. One of the girls went away to Africa so we joined her prayer list. We each have a day to pray for her."

"Also we help two families," says Connie Doyle, another of the Associates.

What were the Sisters like?

Well, for one thing, they weren't like Marilyn imagined them when she was a girl. "When I was growing up, I wasn't the nicest little girl, and my mother would threaten me. 'Straighten up or I'll send you to Maryvale'. And I wasn't the only girl in Windsor who heard that."

"We loved them all," says Connie. "It's hard to pick one over the other. They were so gracious, and such loving people."

"Sister Margaret Mary, she was from Newfoundland," says Marilyn. "My mom was born in Newfoundland. Well, as soon as she found out my mother was a Newfoundlander, we became good buddies. When I went to Newfoundland to visit my brother I called her relatives and she was just thrilled. Newfoundland, to Catholics, is mission territory. When she was growing up she was rarely able to go to mass as the priest visited her community only once a month. And her religious life came out of that."

Connie and Marilyn have covered Connie's kitchen table with snapshots and albums. Marilyn points to one of the photos: "That's Sister Gabrielle. She was a painter. She did beautiful work."

"She made beautiful Christmas cards," says Connie. "She had many orders with regular customers."

What was life like behind the scenes at the convent?

"They were relaxed," says Marilyn. "They would read, and watch TV. They loved to go to the community room and watch *Jeopardy* and *Wheel of Fortune*. They played cards. They listened to music. They had a lot of CDs and the old 78 records. And so many people would just drop in to visit. They would not have their head-dress on. They would wear a casual habit, as opposed to the formal one.

"I remember one time Sister Margaret said 'We're having confession' and I said 'Confession? You guys have confession?' and she said 'Well, yah' and I said 'No way'. She said 'You have a bunch of women living together you can sin.' I said 'Well, I suppose'. I don't suppose they were great sins. But it was something I never forgot. These ten or twelve women living together and praying, what kind of trouble could you get into?

"The number of petitions for prayers was amazing. They had

a bulletin board and they would have notes on there 'So and so called, please pray for them'."

What impact did the Sisters have on the kids?

A little story tells the tale: "When the nuns were leaving, we had a party for them. One of the girls who had been here showed up. After all these years – forty, maybe more – she drove down from Barrie to see them. She just wanted to come back and tell them what a difference they had made in her life."

"Personally," says Marilyn, "I would suspect that children who were cared for at Maryvale would have had a better recovery rate because of the faith and the love of the Sisters. This was the nuns' lives, this was their home, this is all they had to do. The Sisters were totally dedicated to these children's recovery, and I think that made all the difference. They were present. They were on the property. Eight o'clock in the morning, or eight o'clock at night. They were there."

For Marilyn, Sister Anne is the personification of the Sisters. "As soon as she went out the door, if there were any children around they would come right over for a hug. And she always had candies in her pockets. Food for the squirrels, candy for the kids. The kids just loved her."

Of Children and Horses

SISTER VERONICA is 91. She spent more than four decades – most of them at Maryvale – working with young girls. "I worked under Mr. McIsaac. He was a great man. He was great for the girls. He was almost like a father to them. We worked in the convent.

"The girls slept in dormitories. They went to school there. It was a small school, with all the usual subjects: math, English and so on. We took them from the age of 9 and they left when they were about 16. They came from Children's Aid. They were not bad girls. They were children who came from broken homes, perhaps didn't get along with their mothers and so they would come to us and they'd stay until we thought they were ready to go out again.

"We didn't have what you would call street kids. There weren't so many drugs in those days. That really changed things. It was much easier then. These youngsters were just disobedient, or their homes were broken up.

"Everyone had a chore to do, and they had to look after their own room. We had meals from a common kitchen. They had to set the table properly. They had to say grace, and of course you couldn't just jump up from the table and wander around. They weren't a rough bunch, they had some manners, but we just had to put an edge on them.

"We took them on outings. We used to go to Point Pelee. We took our favourite sandwich – baloney and bread, no butter – we called them the Point Pelee sandwiches. We took them to the Detroit Zoo. We went over to Boblo. We took them on many outings.

"In the big house I was the Sister in charge and then when the cottages came in I was in charge of one of them. Each girl was sent to a particular cottage. It seems to me I got all those who didn't like to stay put. There was no fence around the property at that time, even around the yellow building (the convent). There was no fence, but we didn't have too many runaways."

Speaking of which:

"There were four little ones, about 9 years of age, all dressed up for school. They were so clean. I was so proud of them and off they went. Then Sister phoned from school and said these four were not there. I thought 'Oh my gosh, where are they?' I said 'They'll be back because they'll be hungry.'

"Came five o'clock, I saw them across Prince Road where the train tracks are. One was riding a horse and another was hanging on to the tail and the other two were walking beside it, one on each side. I couldn't believe my eyes. They brought the horse right up to the front door. I went out and said 'Where did you get that horse?' and one of the girls said 'It was in an old field out by the Dutch ranch' and I said 'You could be hanged for stealing a horse'.

"I had to call the police when they first went missing, so I called back and said 'I found my girls' and they said 'Oh, where were they?' and I said 'They've stolen a horse'. I could hear them laughing and then I was foolish enough to carry on the conversation and I said 'Yes, and it wasn't a good one at that' and of course they laughed all the harder. The children were still standing there with the horse and I said 'You could get into trouble for this, you're stealing'. 'Oh no, it was in an old field and we took him.' I called the Dutch ranch and told him the girls had stolen his horse and he said 'They did?'. He couldn't even remember the horse. I told him we had it and he came and walked around the horse and he kept saying 'I can't believe it, I can't believe it' and I was telling him 'Make it serious, make it serious'. He said 'I can't believe it' and I wanted to say 'Believe it. Here it is.' Anyway, he took the horse.

"We put the girls to bed. First, of course, we had to give them a bath. They were so dirty. So they went to bed that night and they thought they were off Scot free. I let them go to school next morning and then one by one – I thought I can't tackle them all together – I called them in. I gave them a good talking to and of course made them cry. I said 'You can sit there and cry for a while and once you feel better, you can go back to school,' which they did. And I never saw another horse.

"We had one girl. Her family had lots of money. Her mother used her as a model, she had a modelling school, and the youngster would never wear anything else but a blouse and a blue skirt. She would take them off at night and wash them and put them back on in the morning. She did that for two years.

"Her mother would send her clothes and we never saw them. She just resented being a model. She didn't like being shown off to people. She said she felt like a doll in a suitcase. Her mother would take her out, show her off, and then put her back. She told me one time 'I'm in a deep black hole and I can't get out.' And yet she was a very outgoing youngster as far as we were concerned.

When her mother would visit, she wouldn't have anything to do with her, even in the parlour. Mr. McIsaac did most of the talking, or I did. The girl just sat there with the parcel her mother brought. And I never saw her wear anything other than that blouse and that blue skirt.

"I remember one little blonde one. She was a holy terror. When she first came to me, no one could put up with her. Mr. McIsaac presented her at my door and said 'Will you take her, Sister?' I said 'Fine, but she'll have to understand that she's got to do what she's told'. She looked at me as much as to say 'Try me.' So she came in. I told her 'You have to do the dishes, you have to do a job around the house' and she said 'And what if I don't do the dishes?' I said 'That pile of dishes will still be there in the morning and if they're still there at breakfast, I won't have to say anything, the girls will get after you.' The dishes were done.

"She took temper tantrums."

How would she deal with temper tantrums?

"It was hard. You could hold her, if she'd let you. Or you'd be sure to contain her in her one room because then if she wanted to throw anything she wouldn't dare, because it was hers. But if you let her out, she'd throw anything and break it. So you try to contain her.

"We held them as long as we could and talked to them until they came down. Just holding and talking to them did it mostly, for the little ones anyway. The older ones didn't have so many temper tantrums. They liked to throw things, though. At you, sometimes."

How did she deal with that?

"Ignore it. I've been told to go to hell. I've been told that I'm a bitch. Many times. But I was very protective of my girls, and I think they felt the same about me. If we went on the bus, and girls from another cottage said, 'Here comes the bitch' I wouldn't have to say anything. My girls would take care of things. You certainly needed a sense of humour."

What drew her to this work?

"I was drawn to the Sisters of the Good Shepherd and as you

51

come along they kind of put you where they think you belong. I just fell into it. I was with the girls for probably forty-five years, straight through. All different. I loved it. I feel I fulfilled what I came for."

Do any of the girls still keep in touch?

"Oh yes. One girl kept in touch with me for a long time, one of the nine-year-olds. You remember the ones who made you work hard, you remember them the most."

The Sisters

"THE SISTERS had a profound impact," says Connie Martin. "The people who work here always had tremendous respect and affection for the Sisters. There was one nun, Sister Anne, she just died a year ago, and everyone just loved her. She just had the most bubbly, good-natured, warm personality. She was very effervescent. She was out there because she was dying to see the staff and the kids and chat. There isn't a staff who wouldn't talk about Sister Anne and how much they liked her. So she's almost a ghost in the sense that her presence is still around. You think of her, you look out and you can almost see her hugging some child."

What legacy did they leave behind?

"They symbolized the best of values that people could live by. That's what this place tries to be and that's what the people who stay here buy into. They come in every day and do their best to try to keep it that way. I often think if the Sisters hadn't been here, that foundation wouldn't be here. They started it, they were here and slowly handed it over to lay people and because of them we have a far better chance of keeping those values alive."

1949 – The New Residence

From *A Book of Remembrance, Fifty years of loving labour for the glory of God and the good of mankind 1929 – June 3rd – 1979*

There were about 30 girls in residence when they moved from their cottage (now The Villa) into the new Maryvale building. What exclamations of delighted surprise were heard. "O Mother, isn't it wonderful!" "So big, so bright," etc.

The kind people of Windsor seemed as delighted as we were. They were happy that our dear girls now had a bigger and better "home away from home". Donations of suitable clothes, including evening gowns, were sent in. How the girls loved to get all dressed up and how pretty they looked.

We recall with great gratitude to God how eager the girls were to better themselves. There were many times when, in spite of their best efforts, they would fail; but good will was always there and we found them very responsive.

The Old Windsor Joke

THE PHONE rings at Maryvale. A nun picks up the receiver. "Hello?"

A teenaged voice, male: "Do you save wayward girls?"

"Yes."

"Save one for me. I'll be right over."

Laughter.

Click.

Chicken Heaven

THE SISTERS kept chickens in a coop just east of where the administration building now stands. From Sister Gabrielle's 2007 calendar: (In 1949)

"The gardeners unwittingly threw a pile of weeds close to the chicken coop. Rats moved in and raised families and disturbed the chickens. One evening, the Contemplative Sisters decided to get rid of the rats. They armed themselves with rakes, hoes, sticks, you name it and marched bravely down to the chicken coop. They stationed themselves, like the brave ladies they thought they were, around the pile ... ready for the kill! At the count of three, the leader struck the pile a mighty blow and the rats ran out on every side!!! The brave sisters screamed and ran in every direction. Well, so much for the extermination."

Speaking of extermination: "Thieves stole in at night and carried off the roosters. Hens quit 'work' so ended up on our plates. One of the chickens, Sadie, was antisocial it seems as she flew the coop each day. Consequently, when the slaughter day arrived, she was missing. It was summer, so she was allowed to roam. Sister Catherine fed her every day, but when the cold weather began to settle in, the Superior told one of the Sisters to send Sadie to Chicken Heaven. The cleaver she was given to do this terrible deed was so old, rusty and dull, it couldn't cut hot butter. Okay, Sadie, here goes !!! You can imagine the rest ...."

The Powerhouse For Prayers

"THE SISTERS' commitment was unbelievable," says Frank Chauvin. "When they went in there, they gave up a life. They had no communication with their families. Before they changed the rules, their mother could have died and they weren't allowed to go home. There was one Sister, I forget her name, she was from Vancouver. She wasn't Catholic but she turned Catholic and joined the contemplative order. Her father said 'If you do that, I'll disown you.' She left, she joined the order. Then one day years later they got a call from a lawyer in Vancouver. The father had died and left her the estate which was about sixty thousand dollars. This was fifteen or twenty years ago. So it was a lot of money. The lawyer told her that her father used to brag that he had a daughter who was a nun. She didn't know that. She hadn't communicated with her father since she was a young girl. For 50 or 60 years, she had never seen her father.

"They went in for different reasons. Some of them were sort of pushed into it. They were from religious families where they expected that one of the girls would become a nun. They felt obligated to do it as a sign of respect for their parents. I'm sure some of them didn't really care for it that much. It was an awful life, the contemplative life. It was a real sacrifice.

"When they changed the rules (allowing the nuns to walk around the campus) things were a lot different. I think they were happier.

"But if you wanted your prayers answered, ask the Contemplatives. They had the powerhouse for prayers."

The Contemplative Life

SISTER BERNADETTE entered the convent in 1943 at the age of 21, went to Maryvale in 1972 and stayed there 35 years.

"I was a member of the contemplative community. We had nothing to do with the children. But as time went on and there were changes, we could go out in front of the building on Prince Road and walk around that circular drive and later we were allowed to walk at the back of the house. Sister Anne, she was a great one for hugging everybody. If she saw one of the children, she'd always call them and give them a hug. At that time, we were not supposed to even talk to the staff, never mind the children. But gradually that wore off and we were talking to the children. If they saw us walking by the cottage they would come out, three or four children, and that's where we got the relationship with them. They'd come out and they'd be talking and asking for prayers and they wanted a hug. Some of them would tell us about their families and they would want us to pray for them: this one is having trouble and that one is having trouble.

"The children had their graduation in the chapel and at the end of the ceremony, one of the social workers said 'If you want to greet the Sisters, go on over' and they just flocked over and it was hugging time for all of them. It made a good relationship with them and I think they will carry that in the future: that not all nuns are standoffish. Anne was very friendly with them. We were all friendly, but not as exuberant as Anne.

"So that was all the contact I had, really."

How did she come to this life?

"My mother was having a hard time with me. She was always asking me things, but evidently I was hard of hearing, and mother didn't know – nobody knew that – so she would tell me to do something but I wouldn't know what she was telling me so she thought I was disobedient and being stubborn. She thought she had to do something with me, so she got me into the Good Shepherds. I went into the convent. I was 15 and I was scared stiff.

"I was talking to the Sister and she asked if I could play the piano and I said yes. She said, well you stay there and play the piano, I'm going to vespers – I didn't know what vespers were – and I noticed that when she went out she didn't lock the door and for the first time in my life I felt trusted. I thought, it can't be a bad place here. I think I'm going to like it. I did like it there and I stayed there for about a year and a half. My favourite brother came to see me. He wanted to get married and he wanted me to go home and look after Mother. I said 'I don't want to go home. I like it here and I'm going to stay here until I know what I want to do.' So I stayed there about four years.

"One day I said to one of the Sisters 'Do you think I'd make one of those nuns?' and she said 'Yes, I think you would' and I said 'Oh no, not me' and as I was saying that I heard very distinctly 'I want you.' It was the Spirit talking to me. I thought, you don't argue with the Lord, but Lord I don't want to be a nun. But it kept coming back to me so I thought maybe that's what God wants me to do. I thought maybe I should go home and think about it for a while, to see if it was the right thing; and I don't think I was home half an hour before I knew I didn't want to be there. So I phoned Sister and told her I was coming back."

What's it like, living a cloistered life?

"It was quite cloistered at that time (1943). We worked in the laundry every day and two days a week we worked making scarves. We had a gift shop, we had sewing rooms, we made altar breads and we made vestments and things like that. They were very gifted sisters. They've all gone to Heaven. We were never off the campus. We never went home.

"Our prayer life started first thing in the morning. Around 4:30 A.M. we would go down for half an hour of meditation. Sister would read a point of meditation and then we would all sit there and meditate on that point for half an hour. I had a difficult time because I couldn't hear – I couldn't hear the point of meditation. So the day before I would read something and the next morning I would meditate about that. We had mass at 6 A.M. and then after mass we would go to our work. We were 42 sisters and everybody had a job and we worked until 10:30, dinner was at 11, and then we had an hour of recreation. The first half hour we would go out for a walk and after that we would sit and do handwork (knitting or sewing). Then we would have prayers and go back to work until 3 o'clock.

"At 3 o'clock we would gather together and have a spiritual reading, then we would go down for a cup of coffee or a tea or something, then we'd come back up and say the rosary together. All in all that was about an hour and a half and then we would go back to work and then go to supper. After supper, another walk if you wanted, and then we would go to recreation.

"We did have choir practice once a week and we started an orchestra at one time. We used to have plays and things like that. We could have evening recreations for an hour or an hour and a half. We were always together. My brother used to tell me that he couldn't imagine a bunch of women being together and nobody getting a black eye. We never really had any trouble in that regard. You might get cross with someone, but there were always enough people there that you could go and cool off. At recreation, your name was always on a chair in a group of three. You were always encouraged not to be just two. There was a lot of talk about particular friendships, so maybe that was it, they didn't want us to have particular friendships. Now we're encouraged to talk to each other and we can help each other spiritually, but that wasn't even thought of in those days.

"But we were happy. No black eyes.

"It was a very structured life. You could only have a visit once a month. We could only write three letters a year to our family. When there was sickness in the family, you couldn't go home. If someone died, you couldn't go to the funeral. I didn't go home for my mother or my favourite brother. That was very hard. Then things changed. When my eldest brother died I was able to go to his funeral. It was in Toronto where we grew up. So I said 'I'll see if I can stay at the convent there overnight' and I had all that arranged but my nephew said 'I'd like you to come to the hotel with us.'

"Well, I had never been in a hotel in my life. So the next morning when I got up I got washed and dressed, cleaned up the bathroom the way I always do, made the bed and I was sitting there making my meditation and I heard someone coming in the door. This lady came in and looked at the bed and said 'You made the bed?' and I said, 'Oh, yes, everything's fixed' and she said 'Well, I'll clean the bathroom' and I said 'That's all done too' and I thought 'What's she coming in here for?' Some time later my nephew came in and he said 'Has the maid been in?' I said 'Who's that?' He said 'Who made the bed?' I said 'I did'. He said 'Oh, Aunt Betty...' he got such a kick out of that."

I asked her about the decision to move to the Mother House in Toronto in 2007.

"We worked there (in Windsor) right up until about two years before we came here. Sisters were dying and we couldn't manage all the work. We had ten staff and by the time we paid them and paid all our other bills I knew we weren't going to last very long.

"The Provincial came down and asked how we were going to handle things. We had one sister who had Alzheimer's and I asked the Provincial if she could be moved to Toronto, and that started the rock rolling. When we got down to eight Sisters, I told them we can't go on much longer. At that time, we

James A. McIsaac

thought it was the best thing. We weren't too happy. Change is very difficult. We were accustomed to making our own decisions in Windsor. Here, if you want to do something you have to ask the Superior. We find that hard. But we're all together, that's the big thing."

1950 – James A. McIsaac

JAMES A. McISAAC, first executive director of Maryvale, took up his position here on October 16, 1950 ... only God knows the depth of our gratitude to Jim who worked with us for seventeen years, developing Maryvale's service to teen-aged girls in the Province of Ontario.

Carrying On

THERE WAS no question, in the old days, that Maryvale was a Catholic institution. The crucifixes were one tip-off. So too the statues of Mary. And then, of course, the nuns. "I'm not Catholic," says Janet Glos. "I'd never met any nuns. When I first came I was anxious about that because there was a strong Catholic presence. I wondered 'Am I going to feel I don't fit?'" But shortly after coming, she found that Maryvale's culture made a lot of sense to her. "It's about doing the right things, having certain values, having a commitment to other people. That was really what the Sisters represented to us, those values. We are just carrying on what they started. When you look at the history of the Order, you feel you're carrying on something that's much bigger than yourself. No matter what religion you were, if you shared those values and that commitment, then you felt that passion and that meaning."

Is the Sisters' presence still a felt thing?

"This is just a very different place, a unique place. So yes, I would say we feel their presence very much. All of us still have the lived experience of being with them physically and so it carries on in us."

More Sinned Against Than Sinning

FROM MINUTES of the board meeting June 28th 1951:

"Mother Superior gave us an outline of the Good Shepherd Order as follows: 'The work of the Good Shepherd nuns is to help souls; the work differs with localities. We have schools, hospitals, reformatories, prisons and, as in Windsor, pre-delinquent work, that is, girls with character difficulties for whom the future would seem to be uncertain. Since the foundation of the Windsor house in 1929, nearly 400 girls have been helped. These have been mostly children of broken homes, more sinned against than sinning, and when they have been taught to keep themselves and their surroundings clean and tidy and to maintain a household as a good woman should, we have found that 95% have kept on the right path, being now good happy mothers of families bringing up their own children as assets to society.'"

A New Function

F<small>ROM THE</small> <small>MINUTES</small> of the board meeting November 8th 1951:

"The President introduced Miss Margaret Newton, Field Supervisor of Children's Institutions in Ontario.

"Miss Newton spoke about … the future of the Sisters' present Child Care Program with its emphasis on treatment. She said there is no longer a need for refuges and custodial institutions, but rather the emphasis is put on treatment and rehabilitation in more home-like surroundings. …She spoke of the great need and the new function of Maryvale – caring for adolescent girls with extreme emotional problems, as opposed to the previous function of a refuge giving custodial care. … Miss Newton went on to say that Maryvale is carrying on a unique project in Ontario. At the present time it is the only institution of its kind to serve emotionally disturbed teen-age girls."

Parenting

S<small>OME OF</small> the kids who come to Maryvale have had fabulous parents. Some haven't. But all parents could have used a little help along the way. That's something to which Geralyn LeBlanc devotes a lot of her time and energy. Geralyn is one of the staff who teaches in the Positive Parenting Program.

"When I'm doing the parenting program with parents, I always say I've been blessed to work here because I've got tremendous support, I can bounce questions off anyone, there are many people out there who have no support."

What does psychologist Janet Orchard think of the way we, as a society, raise our kids?

"I don't think we do a very good job, actually. I think the problem is that many people have become disconnected from their family supports. We assume that some innate ability to parent is going to emerge and that everybody should have it and therefore no one has to do anything to remediate it. We do birthing classes, and healthy pregnancy programs; but then it just ends and you go home from the hospital with your baby and somehow have to figure out how to be a parent. I think you go home thinking the kid is going to make you feel good. Yes it does at one level but a lot of times your baby isn't making you feel good: it's crying at three in the morning. I think we do a pretty lousy job of training people how to be parents. I think it would be a fabulous idea to teach parenting in our schools."

Show Me The Money

FROM THE MINUTES of the board meeting December 12th 1951:
"Mr. Wm. Elliott, Chairman of the Finance Committee ... announced that Maryvale is asking the Community Fund for $11,662.07 while our total budget would be $37,662.07 for 1952."

Shepherds and Sheep

GERALYN LeBLANC supervises the boys' residential program in Cottage Five. There can be as many as 10 boys living here. A couple more come in for day programs. The problems? "Quite a range. Some have severe mental difficulties, some can have severe behavioural difficulties, and some have combinations of the two as well as learning difficulties; difficulties with not being able to live at home."

The staff are working with the kids to get through their issues of anger and sadness and resentment and the host of other emotions that lead to the behaviours they exhibit: the behaviours that need changing. "Whatever the difficulties are, we work with them."

While we've been talking, Saint Mary Euphrasia has been looking over Geralyn's shoulder. A picture of the nun who founded the Sisters of the Good Shepherd is thumb-tacked to the bulletin board behind her desk. To her right, there are book-

Rose Virginie Pelletier, later Saint Mary Euphrasia

Saint Mary Euphrasia, foundress of the
Order of the Sisters of the Good Shepherd

shelves crammed with toy stuffed sheep. Geralyn smiles: "It's all about the Sisters of the Good Shepherd. Shepherd, sheep.

"I was here when the Sisters were here. They were on the board and they were around; they lived in the Convent and there were a lot of them. The ones who lived in the Convent were cloistered, couldn't come out; we didn't see them but we knew they were there. We would only see them during chapel services.

"I was lucky to know their presence. I was given the opportunity to meet with the Sisters and four or five other people who belonged to Good Shepherd agencies across Canada. They talked about how we can keep the Good Shepherd values going in these agencies. They were so interested in Maryvale. The big part of what we've helped other people to see is that you can survive without the Sisters but how important is their history, how much are they valued? We want to keep that alive.

"I had the opportunity, along with Carrie (Lee) to go to France, to Angers, to learn so much more about Saint Mary Euphrasia, the history of the Sisters of the Good Shepherd, how she got it started, to know that 300 years ago these Sisters set out in their little wagons, and across the oceans in boats. We found how and when they came to Maryvale, and when they went to different places."

The impact of the Sisters?

"The Contemplative Sisters of the Good Shepherd who were in the Convent, to this day they still pray for the children and for us. That's the whole sheep thing, the shepherd looking over the flock. Taking care of them and nurturing them and healing them. Keeping that alive is very important."

Helping the Helpless

FROM A PAPER delivered in Ottawa, May 1952 by James McIsaac MSW, then Executive Director of Maryvale:

In 1950 Maryvale Vocational School opened its doors to provide a new type of residential treatment project hitherto untried in the Province of Ontario. This program was to consist of specialized educational and social services for 30 adolescent girls who had displayed a significant inability to get along in their own homes or in foster homes. The philosophy behind this new venture was basically one of prevention. All the youngsters admitted during the first two years of operation displayed some form of behavioural difficulty resulting from unsolved anxieties and compulsions which made her adjustment to her own home or foster home impossible.

The School program ranges from Grade Four to Grade Ten. Higher grades are available at local high schools and collegiates. For the girls who are not ready to attend the local school and who have some very real problems around the classroom situation, Maryvale is able to provide some basic vocational subjects which consist of cooking, sewing, an introductory beauty culture course, an elementary course in typing and shorthand and a course in first aid as well as the essentials of home nursing. The counselling services of the Sisters, Priest and Minister are utilized to the fullest. The Sisters who supervise these youngsters are dedicated heart and soul to the rehabilitation of these girls in their care. The Priests and Ministers also provide a spiritual revitalization which is so necessary in so many of our morally mixed-up adolescents.

Fun and Games in the Convent

FRANK CHAUVIN first came to Maryvale back in the 1970s. "After I retired, they were always asking for help because they had no janitor there. I tried to save them as much as I could because they didn't have much money. They were basically living off their pensions. They had no other income apart from the little money they made with their bake sales and craft sales. I used to spend three or four hours in the morning doing odd jobs, fixing sinks, whatever had to be done so they wouldn't have to hire anybody."

"One time Sister Grace said 'Frank, when you get a chance would you check the sink in my room? It's dripping all the time.' So I went up there and sure enough it's dripping and I tried to shut the water off but it hasn't been shut off in twenty years, it's all seized. She's on the third floor. So I go down to the first floor where the shut-off is and I shut the water off and go back upstairs and take the faucet off and put a washer in and put it back together and go back downstairs, turn the water on, go back upstairs, still leaking. So go back downstairs, turn the water off, go back upstairs, fiddle with it some more. And I must have done this five or six times until I finally got it fixed.

"So I was ready to leave and ran into Sister Virginia and she said 'You're still here?' so I told her what I'd been doing, going up and down the stairs, shutting the water off. And she said 'So that's what happened.' The VON had come in and they were going to give this old nun a bath. They got her all undressed and took her in the bathroom and there was no water. So they took her back to her room. Then they went back into the bathroom and there was water. So they went back to her room and they got her and took her back to the bathroom, and there's no water. They did that two or three times and the VON finally gave up. They said 'This place must be haunted. We're not coming back here.' Nobody knew I was shutting the water off. And the old girl never did get her bath."

1962 – The Six Residence Cottages

"A CONTRACT for construction of six cottages at Maryvale Vocational School, Prince Road, has been awarded to A. Lombardo and Son Ltd. The building permit for $561,000 has been approved by the city building department. Each cottage will house 14 adolescent girls and two house mothers and are due for completion Sept. 1."

—From *The Windsor Star*

Lots of Troubles

HUNDREDS AND hundreds of kids have passed through the doors of Maryvale, on the way in, on the way out. It's surprising how many of them make an indelible impression on the staff.

Janet Glos: "We had one fellow who'd been having lots of troubles at home, lots of troubles in schools and right from kindergarten, lots of acting out, not being able to stay in the classroom, suspensions, peer issues. The family had gone through a number of very tragic events. When he came in, the staff spent lots of time playing with him, talking to him, listening to him, communicating to him that we understood what he's been through, what his struggles have been.

"The second step is to look at how much time can this boy handle in the classroom. We could see he could handle up to about 11:30, but after 11:30 he couldn't focus, couldn't do his work, was all over the place. So we had him in school for half a day and in the afternoon we would do other things with him. He did have success and started to feel good about himself. That enhanced his relationship with the teacher and the other staff and he started to think 'I can do well here' and that started to happen.

"A lot of work was done with the family, grief counselling, a lot of support. This boy saw the psychiatrist and they put him on medication and almost immediately he started to say 'I can't believe how different it is, I can't believe how I can sit in my seat, how I can listen, how I can focus.' Within a month and a half he was in class all day and he was doing well and participating. Once we got him in the classroom full-time, trusting and focused, then we really started focusing on the academics he had missed. What are his learning issues, how does he learn? We focused on reading and the basics, like math skills, really trying to make up for lost time.

"In the process of that – learning, feeling successful – the parents started to feel this was going well, that he could be successful. So his home situation improved. He started to get involved in social things. Recently, he's had a bit of a setback, but he came to his social worker, he talked about why he thought that was going on, things got worked out, and in the process we had his medication checked out, he needed more medication, so it's an ongoing process.

"That's just one story."

1964 – More New Buildings

THREE SMILING faces face the camera. The faces belong to Patrick Hucker, vice-chair of the Maryvale board; Raymond Taylor, chair of the board and Mother Mary of St. Margaret. They are smiling, probably, because the photographer from *The Windsor Star* told them to. It's the kind of photo you won't see in *The Windsor Star* these days. It's a sod-turning photo, the kind the paper used to publish as a matter of course. The sod? It's being turned for Maryvale's new administrative complex.

Below the photo, there's a story:

A contract for the construction of a building complex for Maryvale Vocational School, including a chapel, staff residence, administrative offices and school and recreation buildings has been awarded by the Sisters of the Good Shepherd to Meyns Construction Co. of Windsor. Awarding of the contract, which will exceed $700,000 was announced today by Raymond J. Taylor, chair of the Maryvale advisory board and Rev. Mother Mary of St. Margaret, Superior. Ground was broken today and construction is expected to be completed by September 1965.

The new complex consists of an octagonal chapel which is connected to a two-storey staff residence. This, in turn, is connected with an administration wing which joins a classroom wing and recreation wing. The staff residence will replace the old residence which was part of the original Colonel Prince estate.

The school wing includes classroom space and special instruction areas such as sewing and cooking rooms, craft room, conservatory and library. The recreation wing is a combined gymnasium and auditorium, including a swimming pool and related shower and changing facilities.

—*The Windsor Star*, November 21, 1964

I Got Hurt

A. IS 16. He comes to Maryvale twice a week – Tuesdays and Thursdays – after classes end at the community high school he attends. "It's a youth group. It's just where you go and hang out and be with your friends. Some come because parents need time alone. We have a schedule. When we first come here we have a snack and then we go to the lounge and play board games. Then we go to the gym or go swimming until dinner. After dinner, we watch TV and then we go home."

He came to Maryvale in 2006 to go to school. " I was a bit – what's the word? – a bit new, I didn't know the place. I wasn't afraid but it was a shock to be in a new place with new people but after a couple of months they were so nice and so open." He says his time at Maryvale "made me open up, made me talk more. They taught me how to read big books, chapter books, because I didn't like to read chapter books. I liked to read magazines and fiction books, make-believe with pictures and graphics. My social life, I'm more talkative. When I first came here I was, like, caved in.

"I go to a community school from 8 o'clock until 2 o'clock then I come here for the youth group from 2:30 or 3 o'clock until 7:30. School is awesome. I'm in Grade 11. I'm doing math, English, science and cooking. I'm getting a diploma next year.

A. spent three years in a group home before coming to Maryvale. "That was 'cause when I was younger I got hurt by a lot of people. When I was little. Like a lot of times. And my anger, like I did not know how to control it. I'm still talking to a psychiatrist about it. It changed my life. Sometimes I stutter because of it. When I'm trying to think of words, I'm stuttering;

but since I've been talking to a psychiatrist it's a lot better. When I first came here, I was still angry."

Still angry?

"No, not always. It's stupid things, when someone takes something from my room without asking. But not like angry, angry. Just upset."

His is a tough story. "My aunt says she doesn't know how I'm still living. She's surprised that I'm still living because people would just kill themselves if they got hurt like that. But it's done and over with."

Did he ever think of killing himself?

(He shakes his head, no). "It's pointless. You die because of old age or because God wants you to die at a certain point. He put you on this planet for a reason."

Why did He put A. on the planet?

"To change people's lives. I've changed so many people's lives. I taught kids that you can control your anger."

1965 – Sister Mary Immaculate Heart

FROM *The Windsor Star*, August 30, 1965:

Maryvale Vocational School has come a long way since Sister Mary Immaculate Heart Todd of the Sisters of the Good Shepherd helped found it in 1930.

"When we moved here we were told that our convent (the former Essex Golf Club on College Avenue) would stand up only another 10 years. That was 35 years ago. Since its founding, Maryvale has cared for 2,000 homeless girls. The girls, however, moved into bright new cottages at the present site in 1962."

For the past 14 years, Sister has been mistress of a sub-order of the Good Shepherds, the cloistered Sisters of the Cross, comprised of girls once cared for at Maryvale. But for 21 years before that she was director of the school. Dur-

Sister Mary Immaculate Heart

ing that time she did not take a holiday but was with the girls every day.

"I always wanted to work with girls," she explained. "Every girl is likable and they have a good streak and if you touch it, you're there. Many hadn't any attention or love in their lives until they came to us and that's why they are always on the defensive. Before coming here they were urged to be something they weren't because they felt they were never noticed."

The most satisfying part of her work is seeing the success the girls have made of their lives and the happiness that comes with it.

Her "outstanding" work and her love has meant a great deal to the youngsters, said James McIsaac, executive director of Maryvale. She never forgets a birthday or the day the youngsters arrive or leave. Girls at the home echo this praise.

On Monday there will be a reception and tea at the convent and on Tuesday a Mass to celebrate her Golden Jubilee. The reception is being sponsored by the Good Shepherd Ladies' Auxiliary. It will be from 2 until 4 p.m. and from 7 to 9 p.m. at the convent, 3615 College Avenue.

1965 – The Last Christmas in the "Castle"

FROM THE SISTERS' remembrance of the Castle:

On Christmas Eve it was raining and coming down in torrents, too. The Convent was in the most dilapidated state of disrepair one could imagine. Buckets, pots, pans, pails and just about everything and anything was utilized to catch the rain drops from the leaky roof. During the morning a large portion of the kitchen ceiling collapsed in a messy heap on the table and floor. Under the sink a sumac weed squeezed its way into the kitchen through a large crack between the wall and floor. Paint was peeling off everything everywhere. Sister Catherine managed to get the meals somehow amid the buckets and pails. Some Cinderella had the job of emptying the containers as they filled up.

The paint was peeling off the chapel ceiling as well, so Sister Sacristan thought it unseemly to decorate the altar, and Midnight Mass was celebrated without decorations. We planned to give the celebrant a little lunch after Mass, but to our dismay the electricity went off just as Mass ended. So Sister Catherine fried bacon by candlelight, holding an umbrella over herself and the bacon. We retired at last, being lulled to sleep to the tune of rain drops and dreamed of our nice new Convent soon to be occupied by us.

1966 – Demolition of the Castle

From *The Windsor Star*, April 24, 1966:

The one-time home of Colonel John Prince in Sandwich, now part of Windsor, is scheduled for early demolition. Thus will disappear a building of unusual historical significance in the Windsor area. It has served as a convent for the Sisters of the Good Shepherd since 1930. Even at the time of its acquisition by the Sisters from the Essex Golf and Country Club it was a very old building. Now the Sisters, who operate the Maryvale Vocational School for girls, find increased accommodation necessary and look forward to occupying their fine new convent and staff building in the very near future.

Official opening ceremonies were held Sunday afternoon at the new school, administration building, chapel and Sisters' residence at Maryvale Vocational School operated by the Sisters of the Good Shepherd. Opening ceremonies were conducted by Most Rev. G. Emmett Carter, Roman Catholic Bishop of London, Hon. Paul Martin, Canada's minister of external affairs and Mother Mary of St. Margaret, Superior.

Inner Landscapes

Finding Danah Beaulieu is a little tricky. Go past the receptionist's desk, down the hall, turn left, follow that hall, go down a few stairs, take another left, her door is on the left. You won't mistake her office for any other at Maryvale. It's like a miniature artist's studio, which is as it should be, since Danah Beaulieu is Maryvale's art therapist.

Busy young lady. She meets with 23 youngsters individually for about 45 minutes once a week. She also works with three school classes for an hour each week. "Usually in the beginning I do three or four drawing exercises with all the kids. It's fun and it's playful and it gives us a chance to get to know each other." It's an opportunity for Danah to get a sense of the issues the youngsters are dealing with, find out how well they're doing.

"I had a girl last year. I drew a little box and we would pass the page back and forth and we each add something else. So I drew a box and she just went with it and drew boxes and boxes around this box and then she put straight lines through the box so it ended up looking kind of like a web. It showed me how very protected she kept herself and that in order to get to that centre box – to work with her – you had to get through all these boxes. So we had to work with her very slowly and take small steps, really respecting her guard. There are reasons why the kids are here. They've experienced very traumatic things and so they have these guards and we have to respect that."

Do kids ever reveal, through their work, what's inside that final box?

"They can't. A lot of stuff is buried in the unconscious. That's why this art therapy works. It's like the inner landscape coming to life on the page."

Why does art therapy work?

"I think it's because they're at the centre of it. They get to create what they want to create and they can take it at their own pace. I think it's the language of kids: it's colour, it's symbol, it's picture, it's image, it's building things, it's getting their hands busy, it's experimental, it's playful. It makes sense in their world. It lets them be kids."

It helps Danah and the social workers get an understanding of their world as well.

"One of the exercises is called a tree house person drawing. I just say, okay we're going to draw a tree house and a person. And I'll do it too and then afterward we show each other what we drew. One of the boys drew a tree on the left, a house in the middle and then he was on the right hand side. He drew himself inside a little compartment and then he had these spiky things coming at him. He didn't draw himself whole, he drew himself as a stick figure. The first thing that came through to me was the spikes. I thought 'Oh my God, is someone threatening him?' His social worker said he'd gone through a lot of bullying, so he did feel this need to be protected. Something else about that drawing was remarkable: I work with 23 kids and there might be three kids who put themselves in a compartment. That shows me he's very guarded, he's very reluctant to share his emotions. And the stick person spoke a lot to his self-image and his low self-worth, and we're working on that. So all of that came through in his drawing. When he drew the house, he drew a tall door and that tells me you'll gain access to him, you'll be able to have a relationship with him.

"The tree was really interesting. He has really low self-esteem and self-confidence and this showed through in the tree. He's very aloof, very disconnected. It's very hard to make a connection with him. I think he's afraid to do something wrong. But the way he drew the tree, the way he drew the branches and the leaves shows he's starting to come up with the ideas and he's able to bring them to life.

"It's amazing what comes out in one picture."

1967 – More Changes

From *The Annals:*
September 1967 – Mr. McIsaac convalescing after a severe heart attack
September 8 – Mr. Arthur Vossen came to replace Mr. McIsaac
October 31 – Mr. McIsaac officially retired
November 8 – "Mr. McIsaac Night"

From *The Windsor Star,* September 1967:

A native of Saskatoon is the new executive director at Maryvale Vocational School.
Arthur R. Vossen will replace James McIsaac who is

leaving Oct. 1 after serving as director and social worker since 1950.

Mr. Vossen has been executive director of the Catholic Charities of Middlesex County in London since 1965. From 1963 to 1965 Mr. Vossen was a case worker in Calgary with both the Catholic Family Service Bureau and the Jewish Family Service Bureau. Mr. Vossen received his Master of Social Work from St. Patrick's College, Ottawa, in 1961.

1972 – Death of James McIsaac

FROM *The Windsor Star:*

James A. McIsaac died on April 4, 1972. He was 48 years of age.

Professor McIsaac, formerly director of Windsor's Maryvale, was an associate professor in the school of Social Work at the University of Windsor. After spending 16 years at Maryvale, Professor McIsaac was employed by the Windsor Children's Aid Society before going to the university in 1969.

McIsaac House

FITTINGLY ENOUGH, there's a house on campus named in honour of James McIsaac. The building is one of the oldest on campus, dating back to the days when the property was part of the Essex Golf and Country Club. It's a narrow single-storey house, now covered with aluminum siding. There's a partial basement under the rear part of the building, nearest College Avenue and Tom McGuiness begins our tour by taking a visitor around the back of the house, along a pathway made of small concrete stepping stones which he and the boys poured and set in place.

Building little concrete stepping stones is more or less what

McIsaac House painted by Sister Gabrielle Dawdy

Tom and the staff are doing inside McIsaac House. It's a transition home for half a dozen boys who are nearing the end of their stay at Maryvale and it's the job of Tom and the rest of the McIsaac staff to prepare the boys for their move back into the world. The preparation involves all kinds of things – from preparing meals to buying groceries to navigating their way around town on the bus.

It also involves learning some nifty skills, which is why Tom is leading the visitor into the basement. There's the usual assortment of basement stuff in here – bicycles, some tools and, over to one side, some lawn furniture which Tom and the boys have built from cedar and willow they cull from woodlots and ditches. "I like making the rustic furniture and I like gardening. A lot of the boys buy into that type of thing. Not everyone is athletic, not everyone wants to go out and play basketball. Some of them seem to lean more to hands-on projects. So we'll mix a bag of cement and pour some stepping stones."

Pardon the pun, "But it's so concrete for them."

He laughs. "Yes. And they get to see a finished product." It

77

may not seem like a big deal, but building furniture, or fashioning stepping stones out of cement, can do wonders for boys who have not had a lot of success in their lives. "I'd like to say it gives them a little sense of pride, a skill, a little bit of self-worth. It's just hammers and nails, screwdrivers and things. The nail doesn't have to go in straight, it doesn't have to be perfect. Let's just put it together. You'll be the first one to sit on it. If it works, it works. If it doesn't, we'll fix it. It's not a big deal."

For some of these boys, that kind of reaction would come as a surprise. "Maybe all their life things haven't gone right for them. But here it's just another day. Let's just take it one day at a time, one little step. I see them relaxing more. They're not taking life so seriously and I find they're nowhere near as stressed out as when I first got to meet them."

After a tour of the rest of the house, we sit in Tom's office to talk. "We have five boys. They're nice kids. They range in age from 14 to 18 years old and they've been on campus an average of five or six years. They're not old enough, legally, to be in the community on their own yet and they don't have the skills to maintain themselves, financially or emotionally, in the community. They go to school all day and live here. In the summers, they're generally working, either here on campus or we try to help them find something out in the community to just give them a little sense of self-worth. We're teaching them the skills they'll need to live on their own. Everyone has to take a turn cooking one night a week. It's their turn and they have to feed the house. They take a turn once a week going out to get groceries. We talk about budgeting, how to buy groceries, where to get them. If your money runs out, then what do you do? We eat a lot of beans or something. Open the freezer, open the cupboard, let's see what we're going to cook tonight. If they have an idea what they'd like to cook, or a recipe they'd like to try, we'll get the ingredients in."

A typical day at McIsaac?

"The midnight staff gets them up in the morning, gets them through their routines and ready for the day. They'll either go to our school or out to a community school. One of the day staff will take them to the school or out to the buses. So they're gone all day and back here by 3:00 or 3:30. We normally have a coffee or a snack, talk about the day and then the one fellow who has to cook will come up with a menu and we'll help them through that. For the rest of them it's just relaxing time. They can go out and shoot hoops, watch TV, stretch out until meal time. Afterward, everyone has a chore to do: someone will do dishes, someone will clean up. These are things they need to know once they're out on their own."

Many of the graduates from McIsaac House "are out in the community doing quite well, working at grocery stores or gas stations."

How does the staff help the boys deal with the emotional part of leaving, that feeling of not being so secure, or being lonely?

"We talk about things they can do to make themselves feel safe: what is your plan if this, this, or this happens? We tell them that we'll always be here for them and that if there's something they need all they have to do is call. We make sure they have the phone numbers. We keep our door open for them and we keep in contact with them for a year or so. One fellow wanted to come back and do his laundry here for about three years after he moved out. He realized he didn't have to go to the laundromat. He could do his wash and have a coffee here and visit. It was like coming home."

The best part of this program for the kids?

"I think it gives them some self-worth and it's a stabilizing influence in their lives. It gives them some skills so they know they can take care of themselves."

A Short Happy Story

WHAT GOES on in the minds of the staff when they have to open the door and say goodbye?

Geralyn LeBlanc: "I know that we have made an impact with them. They could be the toughest kids or they could be the quietest kid. They call. You may not hear from them for a year and all of a sudden you'll get a call. There's a boy who's birthday is on the same day as mine and every year he calls. And gosh, he's probably 30 now."

My Favourite Place

B. is 17. He's been at Maryvale two years, coming first to the hospital-bed program. "I was so nervous." He worked with the psychiatrist and the other staff for a couple of weeks, then moved to another cottage on campus. "They are awesome staff there." He's gone to school at Maryvale for Grades 9 and 10 and has worked during the summer in the gardens around the campus. After Grade 10 he went back to a community school and now comes to Maryvale two days a week for an after-school program. "There are always friendly people here. This is my favourite place to be."

When I ask him why he likes Maryvale, he says "They helped me learn" and he also likes the food.

How has life changed as a result of being at Maryvale? "I always like to be nice and helpful and I always like to be nice to people." Why is that important? "It's important to me because no matter how different you may seem, there's always a nice side to everyone, I think. And then people will be nice back to you." Not always, however. "Some people tell me to shut up. I don't think that's being nice." Do people pick on him at the community school? "They call me teacher's pet and brown-noser because I always like to help the teacher. That makes me upset."

How does life compare at Maryvale?

"It's different here. They don't call me names."

Does he like being at Maryvale?

"I like the teachers and the staff and the classes have a lot fewer kids and the room is quieter and I can concentrate more on my work. I look forward to being here. I feel more relaxed and calm being here. It helps."

His hopes for the future?

"They say I can stay here until I'm 19. I have one more year of high school then I graduate with my certificate. When I'm done school I'll try to find a job until I'm done college. Then I want to work here."

If that doesn't work out?

"Maybe I can stock shelves at the supermarket."

From The Annals

SEPTEMBER 19, 1973 – Sister Augustine will leave for Toronto in October after forty years in Windsor. She entered here May 15, 1933.

May 1975 – Three canoes were purchased for outdoor education and the summer program.

1976 – End of the Guild

FROM *The Windsor Star* December 10, 1976:

After 35 years of service to the Sisters of the Good Shepherd and Maryvale School, the Good Shepherd Guild will officially disband on Dec. 13 at a Christmas party. When the auxiliary was officially founded in 1941 with Mrs. James Barth serving as president, it was described as a "society of helpers who pledge moral and social assistance to the Sisters who devote their lives and personal service to the upbuilding of character in the young girls under their care."

"There were 25 to 30 women in the guild. Many of the women belonged to the old families of the community," said Mrs. Rosemary Minard, current president. Membership increased steadily until it reached its present figure of 378. Of those, 103 are life members and 45 to 50 are active participants in the guild. "Like many organizations today, we are having problems getting new members," said Mrs. Minard. "Women today have other interests and of course there are great numbers of women who are working and they just don't have the time for volunteer work."

"Over the years, the guild raised between $75,000 and $80,000. A spring tea was held the second Sunday after Easter, then known as Good Shepherd Sunday, at the convent. In the fall, guild members held a card party or bingo in one of the church halls. The guild bazaars also raised large sums of money. The proceeds from these functions went into a general fund to provide treats for the girls. The girls were given Christmas parties complete with gifts, taken on outings to Boblo, the Detroit Zoo, Greenfield Village and other places of interest. Members who had summer homes invited the girls there several times during the summer," said Mrs. Minard.

1983 – Connie Martin

THERE ARE a great many paths leading to Maryvale. This is the path Connie Martin took:

"I think it was meant to be. I left a great job to come down here and a friend sent me the ad for the job at Maryvale and I applied totally out of the blue and got it."

First impressions, coming for the job interview?

"Well, first of all, I'm not Catholic and coming up the walk it didn't take long to sense, oh my, what is this? First of all, it's a huge facility. Secondly it looks like it's very Catholic because there were statues of Mary in the lobby. It was forcing your body to go through something while your mind is saying 'Run, as fast as you can, this is not for you'." She laughs at the memory.

"The receptionist at the time looked like she'd been here for eighty years, probably ran the place, and she looked me up and down and was anything but warm and took me down this hallway that seemed interminable into the convent, put me in a large room and left me there. I remember sitting there for what seemed like forty-five minutes and I literally saw the head of a nun start to come up in the little window in the door, and these eyes just stared at me, and I felt even more like 'this is a crazy place, let me out of here, why am I doing this?' Later I met that nun who was just a dear old thing and she told me they were all dying to see who the candidates were and she was doing her own ranking."

The Last of the Sisters Leave

FROM *The Windsor Star*, Friday June 15, 2007, article by Jessey Bird:

After a quiet goodbye Friday morning, Sister Bernadette, Sister Irene, Sister Margaret Mary, Sister Margaret, Sister Emmeline and Sister Gabrielle gathered their very small amount of personal belongings from their humble living quarters and said goodbye to their home.

"They instilled a spirit into that institution," said Bill MacDonald, who has served on the Maryvale board of directors for more than 20 years. "But as the Sisters age, their head office felt it would be best to bring them all together at their larger home in Toronto. That way, the ones who have become frail can be cared for in a proper manner."

"Our main mission is to pray for the young people," said Sister Bernadette. "We urge them to carry on and have goals."

"They don't teach and they don't proselytize," said Barbara Holmes, who helped look after the Sisters. "What they talk about are the children – how they are and what kind of choices they're making. These are children with all kinds of backgrounds who need a lot of attention. But the respect and the love just pours right out of them for the Sisters because the Sisters love them unconditionally."

"When you came to Maryvale, one of the Sisters became your guardian angel," said 69-year-old Kathyrine Dunn, who was sent to Maryvale at 12 when her mother died. "The Sister who had me was named Sister Veronica. I think

Back row: Sisters Margaret Mary Cooke, Gabrielle Dawdy,
Bernadette Gauer; Front row: Sisters Emmeline Ganter,
Margaret Lahoe, Irene Lacombe

she was worried I would be a hopeless case because I was
such a trouble-maker. We would see them every day walking in the garden and I knew that Veronica was my angel,
but I also knew that I wasn't supposed to talk to her – so I
would just hide in the bushes and talk to her anyway. She
would see me and shake her head – but I just kept on doing
it. If it wasn't for them, who knows where I would be?" said
the retired teacher who travels from Barrie to visit the Sisters about four times a year. "I think those kids are losing a
lot by not having them. There was something about having
the Sisters always there for you when as a foster child you
never felt like your own parents were."

"We were devastated when we heard the news," said
Connie Martin. There is no doubt things will change at

Maryvale. The church will hold services less frequently and despite a photo-filled room that has been created as a tribute to the Sisters, much of the convent will be taken over for other uses.

"Look at this," said Martin, pointing to a tattered paper sign that read: 'Quiet – Prayer Zone'. We're really going to miss them."

Tough Guys

NOT TOO many dry eyes around campus the day the Sisters climbed into the van, took one last tour around campus with the big side door open, then headed down the 401 toward retirement at The Mother House.

Teary eyes, but lots of memories.

Lisa, a supervisor: "When the nuns were still here they would take a little walk around campus at dinner time. When the nuns were out walking on the path, these kids would say 'Oh the Sisters are out there, can I go out and they'd get up from the dinner table and run outside and the Sisters would give them all a hug. They act like they're tough and there they are, running outside to give the Sisters a hug. The chapel services, the same thing. It was that gentle kindness."

The Green Door

THE SISTERS of the Good Shepherd have a long history and that history begins about 200 years ago in a place called Angers, in France. That was the home of Sister Mary Euphrasia, founder of the order. Carrie Lee is one of a number of Maryvale staff who has gone on a pilgrimage to Angers. "It really was life-changing for me. It was a week and a half of intense self-reflection. I had to look at every aspect of myself; learn about Saint Mary Euphrasia, what her mission was and how we could continue it.

"The green door has been there since the building was built;

it's a big green door that leads out onto an alleyway. All these Sisters would come to her to be trained, she would ready them to go out and open up places like Maryvale and she would send them out through this green door and wave goodbye to them on their way to where ever they were going – all parts of the world.

"Our last night there, they brought us into this little room. We sang some hymns and they read some quotes from Saint Mary Euphrasia, all by candlelight and then they sent us out this green door with all these older nuns in their habits waving goodbye to us. And we looked back and there were these Sisters waving. I still get emotional about it.

"I thought, 'This is greater than I ever imagined. I have a responsibility now. I've been taught something. I need to go back and do something with this.' It was an incredibly moving experience."

Connie's Role

JANET GLOS: "She won't want acknowledgement of this, but I've known her since the day she came here, and she has committed herself to this place. And when she leaves, it's going to change. It's about deeply caring for the place."

Carrie Lee: "Connie is a very tough woman. But she doesn't expect anything from any of her staff that she wouldn't do herself. She never runs out of energy. She's always looking out for us."

Little Tiny Memories

WHAT DOES this place mean to the kids once they leave?

Carrie Lee: "I think for some kids, when they first leave, they think 'Thank God I'm not going to be at Maryvale any more'. But over time … I think we give them memories, little tiny memories where they can feel warm and safe."

A Good Place

I ASKED A., the 16-year-old, what he would tell a stranger about Maryvale.

"I would tell them it's a good place to put their kid in because it's an awesome place. Some kids don't like this place because the staff don't treat them like they want to be treated but I think the staff are doing the job they're supposed to. They're trying to make new things happen."

A Happy Ending

NOT EVERY story has a happy ending.

But this one does.

This is D.'s story. She's 16. She lived at Maryvale for two years and is now living back at home, going to a community high school in the morning and Maryvale's school in the afternoon. I asked her how she came to be at Maryvale, what it's been like being here, what kind of help she's been getting, what she thinks of the staff, and what hopes she has for the future.

Here's the transcript of the interview:

Q: What happened in your life that brought you to Maryvale?

A: I had a lot of stuff in my family. In grade school I kinda got in trouble, kinda got kicked out. I didn't really have anywhere else to go. I had a lot of anger. I was so angry all the time. I have a learning disability and at school they didn't understand that I needed extra help. My Grade 7 teacher was the most understanding because he kind of had a feeling that I had something. But nobody else understood me until I came here.

Q: What were you doing to get kicked out of grade school?

A: Throwing tables, chairs. Biting, kicking.

Q: How old were you?

A: From Grades 5 to 7 I was at that school, then it started getting really bad. I'd get frustrated. If a teacher didn't help me I would just walk out of class and get sent to the principal and he would send me back to class and I would walk out again and then I'd get suspended. It was frustrating because my principal didn't understand why I was doing this. So he would suspend me to kind of teach me a lesson, but it didn't. It was hard. Maryvale understands me. In grade school they didn't.

Q: When did you come to Maryvale?

A: I moved in in August 2005 and moved out June 2007. I'm still here but next year I'll be gone for good.

Q: What was it like when you first came here?

A: It was scary. When I first came here I felt abandoned. I thought my mom put me in here because she didn't care about me. But after a while I understood it more. But it was scary. Like, my first day I was really hyper. We have like kids coming in and out all the time. My first two weeks here, there was a lot of stuff going on. I was experiencing how kids behaved when they got mad. It was really loud at night. Kids are screaming and the staff are talking to them. It was scary. And I was like 'why did my mom put me in a place like this?' But then I realized I was one of the people doing that. So I'm doing this too (laughs). So it kind of felt good because there were other people like me and I wasn't the only one flipping out on people. I wasn't the only one struggling in school. I wasn't the only one getting angry for no reason. There's other kids like me. Then again, not everyone has the same issues as me. Other people are in Maryvale for family issues, there are tons of different reasons that kids come here.

Q: You mentioned you had problems with anger. What was making you angry?

A: I don't know. I got angry at people. It's kind of hard to remember a lot of the stuff that happened in the past. I kind of pushed it all behind me and forgot about it. I wanted to feel like a normal kid. I knew I wasn't normal like the kids you see in grade school. I had something wrong. I had some sort of a disability. I had some sort of anger management problems.

Q: What was that like?

A: It was hard. It was scary because when I was in grade school if I did this in front of kids they would, like, not come near me. They'd be, like, wow, she's crazy, get away from me. And still today I talk to some of my friends, kids in my grade school, they're like why were you like that in grade school? I'm like, I dunno. It's the way it was.

Q: What kind of social life did you have in grade school?

A: I didn't have any friends. I never made friends because I was criticized and I was judged.

Q: What happens when you're so isolated as a child and have such a tough time being with other kids?

A: It's tough. You just want to have friends and fit in with other people. Like the popular girls in school. But people just don't notice you. So at recess I would just hang out by myself or with the teachers. It was hard. I just wanted to fit in and be a normal kid. I knew I wasn't. I knew I needed help. I tried talking to kids and they wouldn't talk to me. Like I had so many enemies in grade school. That's why I was so glad to get out of there. Here, everyone's my friend.

Q: Could you tell me how this place has helped you?

A: All the staff here, they're like family. They really helped me. I have really bad anxiety. The social workers made me like a tool box for if I was in trouble. I had a journal in it, and a stress ball, silly putty, so if I was angry I could just clutch it, or write in the journal. If I really hated someone I could write something nasty in my journal. They just helped me come up with so many ways, instead of throwing chairs. They came up with ways: count to ten, listen to my music.

Maryvale, they just helped me a lot. They did so much. When I moved home it was, like, I was a whole new person. I've been home two years now and everything's gone really well. Me and my Mom we have the best relationship. Same with me and my aunt. And I used to hate my aunt. We used to fight over there every day. It's funny because now I'm at my aunt's every day and I used to hate being there. I think part of it was that I used to have to go there. When I had to be there I didn't want to be there.

Q: So you live at home and you come here during the day?

A: Yes. I live at home and then I take the school bus here. Then right at 9 o'clock I walk to my community school and I take my courses there which takes up the morning, it starts at 9 and ends at 11, and then I walk back here and I go to school here in the afternoon. And then I take the school bus home.

Q: What classes do you take here?

A: Right now I'm doing parenting, math and shop. And at the community school I'm doing cosmetology. Next semester I'll be taking hair styling and English.

Q: How do you feel about yourself now, compared with when you first came here?

A: Well when I first came here I wasn't confident. I didn't believe I could do anything that I wanted to do. I didn't put my mind to things. Now, when I look at myself I'm like wow, I'm a completely new person. I'm confident. I grew up to be beautiful, like my Mom. I love music, any instrument. Put any instrument in front of me and I play it. It's just one of my given talents. I'm so confident and so happy with who I am today. I'm so happy that Maryvale gave me this opportunity to change. I'm very sociable – a complete stranger and I'm like 'how's it goin?' – I brighten people's days, that's what people tell me. I make them happy. I put a smile on their face. I'm so happy. I'm so confident now. I know exactly what I'm going to do. I'm going to be a hairstylist.

I've got it all worked out.

GOOD SHEPHERD OVERALL PLAN - 1930-2006

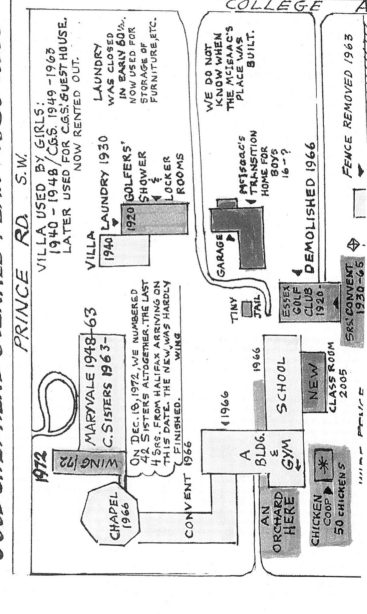

PRINCE RD. S.W.

COLLEGE A

VILLA USED BY GIRLS:
1940-1948 / C.S.S. 1949-1963
LATER USED FOR C.G.S.' GUEST HOUSE.
NOW RENTED OUT.

LAUNDRY WAS CLOSED IN EARLY 60's. NOW USED FOR STORAGE OF FURNITURE, ETC.

VILLA

1940 LAUNDRY 1930

1920 GOLFERS' SHOWER & LOCKER ROOMS

WE DO NOT KNOW WHEN THE MCISAAC'S PLACE WAS BUILT.

GARAGE

McISAAC'S TRANSITION HOME FOR BOYS 16-?

DEMOLISHED 1966

TINY JAIL

ESSEX GOLF CLUB 1920-

SRS' CONVENT 1930-65

FENCE REMOVED 1963

1972

MARYVALE 1948-63
C. SISTERS 1963-

WING '72

On Dec. 18, 1972, we numbered 42 Sisters altogether. The last 4 Srs. from Halifax arriving on this date. The new, was hardly finished.

WING FINISHED 1966

CHAPEL 1966

CONVENT

1966

A BLDG. & GYM

1966

SCHOOL

NEW CLASS ROOM 2005

AN ORCHARD HERE

CHICKEN COOP 50 CHICKENS

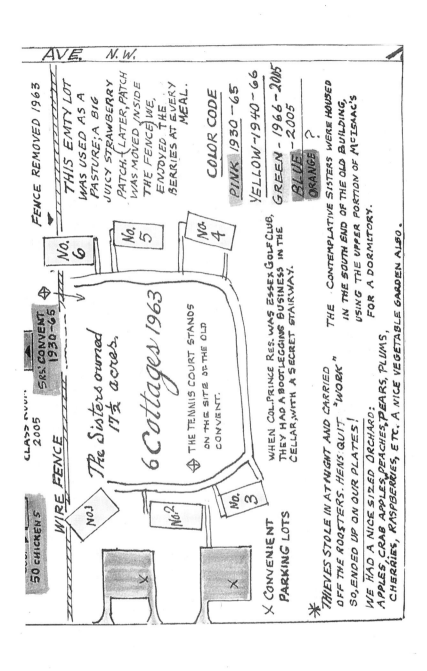

Photo by Dave Chidley

Healing the Hurting is Paul Vasey's tenth published book. Paul is a retired CBC radio morning show host. A newspaperman for twenty five years before making the switch to radio, Vasey has won more than twenty newspaper awards, including the prestigious Southam fellowship for Journalists.

Paul and his wife Marilyn live in Windsor. They have two grown children and two grandchildren. Paul has always been very active with charitable organizations and currently sits on various Boards of Directors.

CRANBERRY TREE PRESS

*The body text of this book was set in Adobe Caslon,
and the section titles were set in Verdana.*

Layout and design of this book was by David Langs.

*This book was printed by Marquis Imprimeur, Inc.
in Quebec, Canada.*